Seventeenth-Century French Drama

Seventeenth-Century French Drama: the Background

JOHN LOUGH

Sometime Professor of French
at the University of Durham

CLARENDON PRESS · OXFORD · 1979

Oxford University Press, Walton Street, Oxford OX2 6DP

OXFORD LONDON GLASGOW NEW YORK
TORONTO MELBOURNE WELLINGTON CAPE TOWN
IBADAN NAIROBI DAR ES SALAAM LUSAKA ADDIS ABABA
KUALA LUMPUR SINGAPORE JAKARTA HONG KONG TOKYO
DELHI BOMBAY CALCUTTA MADRAS KARACHI

© *John Lough 1979*

British Library Cataloguing in Publication Data

Lough, John
    Seventeenth century French drama.
    1. Theater — France — History — 17th century
    I. Title
    792'.0944   PN2632   79-40294

    ISBN 0-19-815756-8
    ISBN 0-19-815757-6 Pbk

*Set by Hope Services, Abingdon
and printed in Great Britain by
Lowe & Brydone Ltd., Thetford, Norfolk*

Preface

After a most inauspicious start the seventeenth century was to prove one of the greatest ages in the history of French drama with the three giants, Corneille, Molière, and Racine. Inevitably not only their plays and those of dozens of other writers of the time, but also the theatrical conditions under which they were produced continue to occupy scholars and critics and to give rise to a never-ending stream of books and articles.

One work that is so far lacking, however, is a short description of the background to this flowering of French drama, particularly in the half century between roughly 1630 and 1680. As this took place almost entirely in Paris, the capital of an already highly centralized country, what the student of the drama of the age needs, after a brief glance at what was happening in the provinces, is a short account of such matters as the theatres of the capital and the companies which played in them; the lot of the actor and the playwright (sometimes, as with Molière, one and the same person); the sort of spectators who were present at theatrical performances; the stage settings and costumes used in this period; and finally the famous Rules which so greatly influenced French drama from the 1630s onwards.

In seeking to fill this gap the present work does not aim at propounding novel theories on any of these questions. Its purpose is rather to summarise the present state of knowledge and to distinguish between what is solidly established and what, for want of clear evidence, must remain more or less conjectural. Its debt to numerous books and articles published during the last hundred years will be obvious to any specialist who happens to open its pages, and, needless to say, it is made clear both in the notes and bibliography. The last chapter is particularly indebted to *La Dramaturgie classique en France* of Professor

Jacques Scherer.

Professor P.J. Yarrow of the University of Newcastle upon Tyne read the manuscript and offered a number of valuable suggestions which have found their way into the text. I am greatly indebted to him and also to Professor W.B. Fisher of the Department of Geography of this university to whom I owe the map showing the position of the principal Paris theatres in the seventeenth century.

J.L.

Durham
March 1977

Contents

Introduction: Paris and the provinces

Although most of this book is devoted to theatrical activity in Paris, it must not be thought that in seventeenth-century France the provinces played an absolutely insignificant part in this field. Indeed in the opening decades of the period when, as we shall see, Paris lacked even one permanent theatre company, the provinces (and to some extent such foreign countries as the Netherlands and Germany) provided a refuge for those troupes which tried, but failed to establish themselves in the capital. Throughout the century numerous companies of actors toured the provinces as well as neighbouring countries. The most famous of these is, of course, the one joined by Molière and his companions in the 1640s after the collapse of the Illustre Théâtre which had been unable to stand up to the competition of the two companies already in Paris. It was not until 1658 that he was able to establish his company in the capital. Many other actors of the time, including some of the most famous, began their career in a provincial company and only gradually succeeded in securing a foothold in one of the Paris theatres.

In the last hundred years a great deal of work has been put into the study of provincial archives in an endeavour to track down the presence of theatre companies in towns and cities. The results of these researches, though inevitably very incomplete, are interesting so far as they go. They are neatly summed up in the invaluable *Dictionnaire biographique des comédiens français du XVIIe siècle* of Georges Mongrédien.[1] The number of times the presence of theatre companies is recorded for the towns and cities of the northern half of the country in the period 1590—1710 is as follows:

---

[1] Paris, 1961, p.10. See also the *Supplément* to this work by G. Mongrédien and J. Robert (Paris, 1971).

Dijon	72	Lille	48
Lyons	57	Metz	27
Nantes	53	Poitiers	20
Rouen	51	Nancy	19

These figures are obviously only a very rough indication of the amount of theatrical activity in these towns and cities. Rouen seems to have been particularly important for a good part of the century. Indeed in the opening decades of our period a great many new plays were first published there and not, as one might expect, in Paris, the natural centre of the book trade of a highly centralized country. It may well be that the frequent appearance of touring companies in that city encouraged the young poet, Pierre Corneille, to turn to writing plays.

In contrast, even though Molière and his company spent a considerable part of their years in the provinces in the towns and cities of the southern half of the kingdom, these would appear to have offered much less scope for strolling players, perhaps partly because of the linguistic barrier presented by the tenacity with which the Occitan dialects continued to be spoken. The number of visits paid to these towns and cities by companies of actors recorded for the same period is noticeably smaller than for those in the northern half of the country:

Marseilles	22	Carcassonne	4
Bordeaux	21	Toulon	4
Toulouse	11	Bayonne	4
Agen	6	Béziers	3
Narbonne	5	Albi	2
La Rochelle	5	Castres	1
Pézenas	4	Pau	1
Avignon	4		

Yet, despite the considerable amount of information assembled by a variety of scholars, the plain fact of the matter is that we know singularly little about such vital matters as the repertoire of these provincial companies, the kind of improvised theatres in which they performed, the financial problems which they had to face, or the sort of spectators whom they attracted to their performances. Endeavours have been made to fill in these gaps, particularly for Molière's company, by reference to a well-known novel of the period, Scarron's *Roman comique*, the two parts of which appeared in 1651 and 1657 at the very time when it was touring the provinces. But while it is possible, given some knowledge of theatrical conditions in this period, to glean from this novel some hints as to what the life of a touring company was like, the general tone of this often burlesque work prevents the modern reader from accepting it as giving a reliable picture. Inevitably there remain huge gaps in our knowledge of theatrical activity in the provinces in the seventeenth century.

It must be said that the same is also true of what was going on in Paris in the opening decades of the century. There is, to begin with, the odd fact that until the 1630s — at a time when Shakespeare and the other Elizabethan dramatists in England and playwrights like Lope de Vega and Calderon in Spain were producing works which are very much alive centuries later — French playwrights produced not a single work which still holds the stage. The great flowering of French drama was only to begin about the end of the third decade of the century. Despite the labours of modern scholars there are for this earlier period great gaps in our knowledge of the activities of the succession of theatrical companies — Italian and even English as well as French — which appeared in Paris in these years, nor do we know in any sort of detail what sort of plays they performed, what stage settings they employed, or the kind of spectators they succeeded in attracting to their performances. What is, however, clear is that the theatre was not yet the fashionable form of entertainment which is was to become from about 1630 onwards; this is made clear by the short stays made by the series of French companies which came in from the provinces, only to depart again, often laden with debts. What is more, it was not until about 1630 that the famous Rules which we associate with seventeenth-century French drama and which were to effect a complete transformation in the kind of plays produced from then onwards, began to be argued over by the critics and very gradually applied by the new generation of playwrights which appeared on the scene at this point.

This new generation of playwrights among whom Pierre Corneille was only slowly to emerge as the leading figure found aristocratic patrons, starting with Cardinal Richelieu, to support them and to raise them above the status of a mere hireling of the actors, a *poète à gages*. Not only was one company of actors permanently installed at the Hôtel de Bourgogne in 1629 but Paris now acquired a second company which, from 1634 onwards, was established in its own theatre, the Théâtre du Marais. Unquestionably the theatre had become a much more fashionable form of entertainment than in the earlier decades of the century, though whether this also involved considerable changes in the social composition of theatre audiences is one of those questions about which scholars argue simply because the available evidence is far too scrappy to make clear judgements possible. What is beyond question is that the theatre in Paris had entered on a new phase. In the capital were assembled the best playwrights and the best actors. It was here that in the following fifty years the drama was to be carried to astonishing heights. The chapters which follow will therefore concentrate on the theatrical life of the capital.

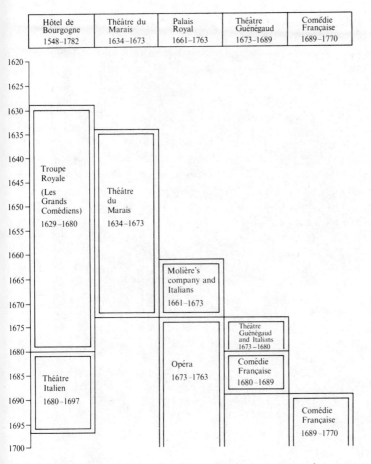

Hôtel de Bourgogne 1548–1782	Théâtre du Marais 1634–1673	Palais Royal 1661–1763	Théâtre Guénégaud 1673–1689	Comédie Française 1689–1770
1620 **1625** **1630** **1635** **1640** **1645** Troupe Royale (Les Grands Comédiens) 1629–1680 **1650** **1655** **1660** **1665** **1670** **1675** **1680** Théâtre Italien 1680–1697 **1685** **1690** **1695** **1700**	Théâtre du Marais 1634–1673	Molière's company and Italians 1661–1673 Opéra 1673–1763	Théâtre Guénégaud and Italians 1673–1680 Comédie Française 1680–1689	Comédie Française 1689–1770

The principal theatres and companies in seventeenth-century Paris

A map of seventeenth-century Paris showing the approximate position of the principal theatres

1 Théâtre du Marais   2 Hôtel de Bourgogne   3 Palais Royal   4 Théâtre Guénégaud   5 Comédie Française
A Notre Dame B The Louvre

1 Paris theatres and companies

At the beginning of the seventeenth century Paris had only one purpose-built theatre. This was the Hôtel de Bourgogne, situated at the junction of the Rue Mauconseil and the Rue Française on the site of what is now No. 29 Rue Étienne-Marcel; it had been built in 1548 on ground previously occupied by a mansion of that name. It was the property of the Confrérie de la Passion, an association of Paris tradesmen which since the fourteenth century had existed to perform mysteries, particularly the *Mystère de la Passion*. In that year the Paris Parlement confirmed its monopoly of theatrical performances in the capital and its suburbs, but forbade it to perform any more mysteries. Before the seventeenth century began, these amateur actors had given up performing plays themselves and had begun to hire out their theatre to such companies of professional actors as came in from the provinces or from further afield, from such countries as Italy or even England. Simultaneously they endeavoured to enforce their monopoly of theatrical performances in the capital by prosecuting companies which performed in improvised theatres in other parts of the city and obtaining payment from them.

From 1600 down to 1629 no company of actors was permanently installed at the Hôtel de Bourgogne. All sorts of companies came and signed leases of the theatre and then departed again, often burdened with debts. During the last hundred years the efforts of a succession of scholars have produced a fairly detailed account of the series of occupants of the theatre during the first three decades of the century, but there are still gaps in our knowledge, and consequently there is some degree of uncertainty as to whether it was occupied during at least some of them by companies of actors, known or unknown. Most of the companies stayed only for a short time, often for a period of weeks or at most months, though by the middle of the 1620s leases were tending to get longer.

It was not, however, until the end of 1629 that the Hôtel de Bourgogne came to be occupied by one company of actors exclusively. An *arrêt du Conseil* assigned the theatre for a period of three years to the Troupe Royale—'les Grands Comédiens' as they were sometimes called. This lease continued to be renewed thereafter at fairly regular intervals until in 1680 this company was merged with the other French actors to form the Comédie Française. This was the theatre in which most of Racine's tragedies and his one comedy were first performed; its actors were the chief competitors of Molière and his company when they returned to Paris in 1658 and were consequently satirized in his little one-act comedy, *L'Impromptu du Versailles*, composed during the controversy stirred up by the phenomenal success of *L'École des femmes*.

When the Troupe Royale vacated the Hôtel de Bourgogne in 1680,[1] the theatre was handed over to the Italian actors. A number of different Italian companies had performed in Paris for the court and often also at the Hôtel de Bourgogne down to the mid-1620s. Another company arrived in 1639 for a much longer stay than usual, remaining until the outbreak of the civil war of the Fronde in 1648. When it was over, in 1653, a fresh company arrived with the famous actors, Scaramouche and Trivelin. On its return to Paris, Molière's company shared two successive theatres with the Italian actors who also shared a third theatre with the new French troupe formed after his death. The Italians performed at the Hôtel de Bourgogne from 1680 to 1697 when they were expelled by Louis XIV, probably for putting on a play which was held to contain allusions to his morganatic wife, Mme de Maintenon. However, this theatre building was to have a long life; in 1716 the Italian actors were recalled by the Regent, Philippe d'Orléans, and they returned to their old theatre which they continued to occupy until in 1783 they moved into a new building which gave its name to the Boulevard des Italiens.

In 1634 Paris acquired its second established company of actors; a troupe which had arrived from the provinces four years earlier installed itself in the Théâtre du Marais, situated

---

[1] In 1677 the Confrérie de la Passion was dissolved by a royal decree and its property was handed over to the Hôpital Général.

in the Rue Vieille du Temple (now No. 90) in a *jeu de paume* converted for permanent use. Before moving into this theatre, the company had begun, as was common at the time (that is how Molière's company was to begin its career in 1643), by performing in a succession of *jeux de paume*, that is, courts for a form of indoor tennis which because of their size and oblong shape could be quickly adapted, either temporarily or permanently, for theatrical purposes. After a disastrous fire in 1644 the theatre had to be rebuilt; this gave it for a while a more up-to-date stage and auditorium than those of the Hôtel de Bourgogne, so much so that when, three years later, the Troupe Royale at last persuaded the Confrérie de la Passion to modernize its theatre, the contract for the building work laid it down that it was to be carried out 'à l'instar et conformément aux théâtre, loges et galeries qui sont au jeu de paume du Marais où représentent des comédiens'.[1]

The Théâtre du Marais had a somewhat chequered career between 1634 and its final abandonment in 1673 when the company performing there was amalgamated with the remnants of Molière's company after his sudden death. It had at times some very distinguished actors, starting with the famous Mondory who scored a tremendous success in the role of Rodrigue in *Le Cid*. It was indeed at this theatre that all the early plays of Pierre Corneille were performed, though later in his career he was to offer some of his works to rival companies, both the Grands Comédiens at the Hôtel de Bourgogne and that of Molière. On a number of occasions some of the leading actors of the Théâtre du Marais were compelled by royal command to move over to the Hôtel de Bourgogne, and for various reasons (one of them was its distance from the centre) it also had lean years and indeed at times it remained closed while the actors went off to perform in provincial centres such as Rouen. In the second half of its existence the company scored its main successes with what were called *pièces à machines,* plays with a large spectacular element.

The Illustre Théâtre which Madeleine Béjart and Molière founded in 1643 began its career in Paris, first in one, then in

---

[1] S.W. Deierkauf-Holsboer, *Le Théâtre de l'Hôtel de Bourgogne* (Paris, 1968–70, 2 vols.), vol.ii, p.185.

another converted *jeu de paume*, but it failed to secure a foot-hold in the capital against the competition of the two rival theatres at the Hôtel de Bourgogne and the Marais. Molière and his companions were compelled to spend a long period as strolling players in the provinces before they were at last able to return to Paris in 1658. On their arrival, after winning the favour of Louis XIV, they were allowed to establish themselves in the capital and to share with the Italian actors the theatre in the Hôtel de Petit-Bourbon, on part of the site soon to be occupied by the colonnade at the east end of the Louvre. When this playhouse was suddenly demolished two years later, the two companies were homeless. However, in the long run they did well out of this forced move. The palace which Richelieu had built for himself and which he bequeathed to Louis XIII (hence its change of name from Palais Cardinal to Palais Royal) contained a fine theatre, inaugurated in 1641, not long before his death. Molière's company and the Italians were allowed to take over this building (long since demolished), situated on the south-east corner of the present palace along the edge of what is now the Rue de Valois. It was there that, from January 1661 onwards, most of Molière's plays received their first performance, but when he died in 1673, the theatre was taken over by Lulli for his recently founded Opéra which was to remain there until 1763.

The remnants of Molière's company were then amalgamated, as we have seen, with the company at the Théâtre du Marais. The new company took over the theatre of the Hôtel Guénégaud (now No. 42 Rue Mazarine) which had been opened in 1671 to house the Opéra; this meant a move to the left bank of the Seine. The Italian actors continued to share this theatre as they had done with Molière's company. When in 1680 Louis XIV forced an amalgamation of the Théâtre Guénégaud and the Grands Comédiens to form the Comédie Française, the Hôtel de Bourgogne was handed over to the Italians, and the Théâtre Guénégaud continued to be used by the new company until it was compelled to move from this building and seek a new site. In 1689, after many vain attempts to find a place where the clergy did not object to its presence, the Comédie Française finally ended up on the same side of the river, only some two hundred yards away, in the Rue des Fossés Saint-Germain, now known as the Rue de l'Ancienne Comédie, where the façade of its theatre can still be clearly seen at No. 14. There it was to remain until 1770.[1]

Although in 1700 Paris had, apart from the Opéra, only one permanent theatre and one company of French actors, there is no question but that in the course of the seventeenth century drama had made enormous strides, particularly from the 1630s onwards. The one company at the Comédie Française was large enough to offer performances not just for two or three days in the week, but every day of the year apart from the usual Easter break, and at the same time to give court performances at Versailles or Fontainebleau. It was thus the equivalent of at least two of the companies which had flourished in the period between 1630 and 1680. Since the 1630s Paris had enjoyed the privilege of seeing on the stage a series of brilliant actors and actresses in both comedy and tragedy. A century which had begun with the most dismal conditions in the theatre was gradually to see one of the most brilliant ages of French drama with the emergence of the three great figures of Corneille, Molière, and Racine.

In considering the lot of the actor in our period we have to bear in mind that it was only in the second half of the sixteenth century that companies of professional actors began to emerge in France as in other Western European countries. Indeed actresses appear to have been few in number at the beginning of the seventeenth century, and in comedy and farce female parts were often taken by men. Thus the role of the *nourrice* in Corneille's first two comedies seems to have been played by a man, while it is certain that this was the case several decades later with such female parts in Molière's comedies as Madame Pernelle in *Tartuffe* and Madame Jourdain in *Le Bourgeois Gentilhomme*; even the part of Philaminte in *Les Femmes savantes* appears to have been treated this way. By this date,

---

[1] After a period of twelve years during which the Comédie Française performed in the Tuileries palace, in 1782 it moved to a newly built theatre on the site of the present Odéon. Its present theatre next to the Palais Royal on the other side of the Seine was built for another company shortly before the Revolution.

however, this was done not because of any shortage of actresses, but for comic effect.

Rare as actresses may have been at the beginning of the century, they were not unknown as they were on the Elizabethan and Jacobean stage. When a French touring company visited London in 1629, the presence of women on the stage was one of the things which shocked the contemporary who wrote: 'Last daye certaine vagrant French players, who had beene expelled from their owne contrey, *and those women*, did attempt, thereby giving just offence to all vertuous and well-disposed persons in this town, to act a certain lascivious and unchaste comedye, in the French tonge at the Blackfryers.' Not without some exaggeration, perhaps, he thus describes their reception: 'Glad I am to saye they were hissed, hooted and pippin-pelted from the stage.'[1] In contrast in Paris for aesthetic and other reasons actresses were quickly to constitute one of the main attractions of the theatre as it gradually became a fashionable form of entertainment.

The fragmentary evidence at our disposal concerning the companies of actors which came to perform in Paris in the opening decades of the century would seem to indicate that their financial position was extremely precarious. Box office receipts were generally poor, and the rent of the Hôtel de Bourgogne was a heavy charge on their takings. Their stay in the capital was almost invariably short; they were often unable to pay the debts which they had contracted and were soon compelled to leave the capital for the provinces or for foreign parts. If they attempted to find a cheaper place to perform in, they were promptly prosecuted by the Confrérie de la Passion and made to pay up. One must beware of taking too literally the oft-quoted passage from the *Historiettes* of Tallemant des Réaux (after all, he was not born until 1619), but there must be some truth in what he wrote of the position of actors at the end of the sixteenth century and in the opening years of the seventeenth:

Agnan a été le premier qui ait eu de la réputation à Paris. En ce temps-là les comédiens louaient des habits à la friperie; ils étaient vêtus infâmement,

---

[1] G.E. Bentley, *The Jacobean and Caroline Stage. Dramatic Companies and Players* (Oxford, 1941, 2 vols.), vol.i, p.25.

et me savaoemt ce qi'ils faisaient.

Depuis vint Valleran qui était un grand homme de bonne mine; il était chef de la troupe; il [ne] savait que donner à chacun de ses acteurs, et il recevait l'argent lui-même à la porte . . . Il y avait deux troupes alors à Paris; c'étaient presque tous filous, et leurs femmes vivaient dans la plus grande licence du monde; c'étaient des femmes communes, et même aux comédiens de la troupe dont elles n'étaient pas.[1]

Certainly by the 1630s, even if the morals of actresses were to continue to furnish material for the *chronique scandaleuse*, the financial position and social standing of the profession had greatly improved and this process was to continue as the century wore on.

However, before examining these developments we ought first to consider how companies of actors were organized in this period. Here we can obtain valuable guidance from the documents which modern scholars have dug out of the archives and from a contemporary source, *Le Théâtre français,* published in 1674 by a minor writer named Samuel Chappuzeau. When a new company was formed either in Paris or the provinces, the actors went along to a notary and drew up a formal contract defining the duration of the agreement and the duties of those signing it. As these contracts were always for a limited period of time, fresh ones had to be drawn up every now and again by companies such as the Troupe Royale at the Hôtel de Bourgogne which had a long career. During the last hundred years quite a number of such agreements have been exhumed from the archives of France. As an example (chosen for its relative brevity) we may take the contract by which this company renewed its association in 1642 for a further five years. The archaic legal French cannot easily be modernized and is therefore left in its original state:

Furent presens en leurs personnes Pierre Messié, s^r de Bellerose, damoiselle Nicolle Gassot, sa femme, Claude Deschamps, s^r de Villiers, damoiselle Marguerite Beguin, sa femme, Zacarie Jacob, dit Montfleury, damoiselle Jehanne de la Chappe, sa femme, André Boiron dit le Baron, damoiselle Jehanne Ansoult, sa femme, François Chastelet, s^r de Beauchasteau, damoiselle Magdelaine du Pouget, sa femme, et Bertheran de Sainct Jacques, tous commediens du roy, lesdictes femmes de leurdictz maris authorisée pour l'effect des presentes et dependances, lesquelles partyes

---

[1] Tallemant des Réaux, *Historiettes*, ed. G. Mongrédien (Paris, 1932-1934, 8 vols.), vol. vii, p.121.

par le commandement de sad. Majesté se sont associez et associent par ces presentes l'un avec l'aultre sans augmenter aulcun personnage avec eulx sy ce n'est d'un commung consentement pour faire la commedie ensemblement pendant le temps de cinq années qui commenceront au jour et feste de Pasques prochain venant sans interruption, ladicte societté ainsi faicte à la charge de payer par celluy qui s'en voudra departir aux aultres ou au porteur des presentes lettres pour eulx incontinant lad. contravention, la somme de mil livres tournoiz de peyne commise et stipulée entre eulx sans aulcune formalité de justice sur ce garder. Car ainsy etc, promectant etc, obligeant chacun en droict soy etc le mary avec la femme sollidairement sans division ne discution, renonceant de part et d'autre mesmes ausdictz beneffices et exceptions d'iceulx. Faict et passé à Paris en la maison ou lesdictz sᵣ et damoiselle de Belleroze sont demourantz rue Mauconseil paroisse Sainct Eustache l'an mil six cens quarante deux le unzeiesme jour de janvier apres midy et ont signé ces presentes subjettes au scellés.

Deschamps	Le Messier	Boyron
Margueritte Beguin	Nicole Gassot	
F. Chastelet	J. Ansout	Zacarie Jacob
Madelaine du Pouget	Jeanne de la Chappe	
	B.H. de Sᵗ Jacques	
		Desprez[1]

It will be noticed that this agreement contains the usual clause exacting a stiff penalty—in this case 1,000 livres—from any member of the company who left it before the end of the stipulated period.

The affairs of the company were dealt with in a democratic fashion, one in which the women members played their part equally with men. There were naturally differences in the share of the individual members in the earnings of the company; while the experienced and skilful actor or actress would receive a full share, the beginner would start with only a quarter and would hope in time to graduate through a half-share and a three-quarter-share to a full share. Even if, as was the case with Molière's company, there was an obvious leader, he did not earn more than its best-paid actors. Some months before Molière's marriage La Grange made the following entry in his register: 'Monsieur de Molière demanda deux parts au lieu d'une qu'il avait. La troupe [les] lui accorda pour lui ou pour sa femme s'il se mariait.'[2] Actors and actresses became a very closely knit

---

[1]   S.W. Deierkauf-Holsboer, *Le Théâtre du Marais* (Paris, 1954–58, 2 vols.), vol.i, pp. 182–3.

[2]   *Registre*, ed. B.E. and G.P. Young (Paris, 1947, 2 vols.), vol.i, p.33.

community, intermarrying on a considerable scale with conse-
quences which Chappuzeau points out:

Quelquefois la demi-part et même la part entière est accordée à la femme
en considération du mari, et quelquefois au mari en considération de la
femme; et autant qu'il est possible, un habile comédien qui se marie prend
une femme qui puisse comme lui mériter sa part. Elle en est plus honorée,
elle a sa voix dans toutes les délibérations, et parle haut, s'il est nécessaire,
et (ce qui est le principal) le ménage en a plus d'union et de profit. Il en est
de même d'une bonne comédienne, à qui il est avantageux d'avoir un mari
capable et qui ait acquis de la réputation.[1]

Inevitably this democratic form of government could not
always prevent dissensions within the company as a result of
which one or more actors withdrew and, so long as the presence
of two or more troupes in the capital made this possible, joined
a rival company. Until the reduction of the French companies
to one in 1680 such changes were quite frequent. Thus Made-
moiselle Du Parc, Racine's mistress, followed him to the Hôtel
de Bourgogne when he had abandoned Molière and transferred
his second tragedy, *Alexandre,* to this theatre.

Sometimes these changes were not voluntary, but were
produced by government intervention. Twice, in 1634 and again
in 1642, a royal decree compelled the Théâtre du Marais to give
up some of its best actors to the Hôtel de Bourgogne. Just as
permission to perform in a provincial town had to be sought
from the local authorities, in Paris companies could only
establish themselves by permission of the king. If in 1629 the
Troupe Royale was able to install itself permanently at the
Hôtel de Bourgogne, this was because an *arrêt du Conseil*
decreed that this theatre should be assigned to them. When
Molière and his company returned to Paris in 1658, after their
first performance before Louis XIV at the Louvre, 'Sa Majesté',
according to the preface to the 1682 edition of his works,
'donna ses ordres pour établir sa troupe à Paris.' However, the
royal authority could also be used to put an end to the existence
of a company. When Molière died fifteen years later, Louis XIV
closed down the Théâtre du Marais and united its actors with
what remained of Molière's company, gave the Palais Royal
theatre to Lulli for his Opéra and compelled the new company
to seek other quarters. In 1680 he decreed a union between

[1] *Le Théâtre français,* ed. G. Monval (Paris, 1876), p.98.

the Troupe Royale at the Hôtel de Bourgogne and the Troupe du Roi at the Théâtre Guénégaud to form the Comédie Française, thus eliminating all competition between rival French companies, and in 1697 he ordered the expulsion of the Italian actors from France.

Although the actors of the Comédie Française still retained democratic forms of self-government, they had now become very much a State enterprise, one which until the Revolution was placed under the authority of the Gentilshommes de la Chambre who intervened in all sorts of matters such as the engagement of new actors, the size of their *part* and even the acceptance or rejection of plays. Undoubtedly the actors lost a great deal of their former freedom to conduct their affairs in their own way.

It can well be imagined that in the age of Absolutism neither actors nor playwrights were free to put anything they liked on the stage without hindrance from the authorities. However, the various forms which this censorship took are not easily set forth owing to the penury of documents. For instance, in 1619 the Paris *Lieutenant civil* issued a decree concerning actors which contained the clause: 'Leur défendons de représenter aucunes comédies ou farces qu'ils ne les aient communiquées au procureur du Roi et que leur rôle ou registre ne soit de nous signé.'[1] However, this appears to have remained a dead letter, and it was not until the beginning of the eighteenth century that a regular theatre censorship was established; but this was far from meaning that at any period in the century the actors were free to put on what they liked.

The Paris lawcourts continued to exercise control over the plays which they performed. In 1624, for instance, the Châtelet, on learning that a company of actors at the Hôtel de Bourgogne (perhaps the future Troupe royale) had put up posters announcing the performance of a satirical comedy which made fun of *commissaires de police*, ordered that 'lesdits comédiens seront pris au corps, amenés prisonniers ès prisons de la cour'.[2] Again it was the *Premier Président* of the Paris Parlement who, in the absence of Louis XIV at the front, banned the performance of

[1] N. de Lamare, *Traité de la police* (Paris, 1705-38, 4 vols.). vol.i, p.440.
[2] E. Campardon, *Les Comédiens du Roi de la Troupe française pendant les deux derniers siècles* (Paris, 1879), p.278.

the revised version of *Tartuffe* which Molière put on in 1667. It was, however, more and more the government which took steps to ban plays, generally after one or more performances of them had been given, though exactly how it operated in such cases is often obscure. Thus in 1665 after quite a successful run before the Easter break, Molière's *Dom Juan* did not reappear on the stage either after it or indeed on any occasion during his lifetime; nor was it ever published by him. Here government intervention must be assumed but cannot be proved. We also know that from time to time the king issued warnings to the actors about their alleged indecent postures and expressions; the Italians had been rash enough to ignore such warnings before their expulsion from France.

The share to be received by each individual actor was determined and paid over immediately the performance had ended, as Chappuzeau indicates:

La comédie[1] achevée et le monde retiré, les comédiens font tous les soirs le compte de la recette du jour, où chacun peut assister, mais où d'office doivent se trouver le trésorier, le secrétaire et le contrôleur,[2] l'argent leur étant apporté par le receveur du bureau, comme il se verra plus bas. L'argent compté, on lève d'abord les frais journaliers; et quelquefois en de certains cas, ou pour acquitter une dette peu à peu, ou pour faire quelque avance nécessaire, on lève ensuite la somme qu'on a réglée. Ces articles mis à part, ce qui reste de liquide est partagé sur-le-champ, et chacun emporte ce qui lui convient.[3]

In the last act of Corneille's baroque play, *L'Illusion comique*, probably first performed in 1635,[4] the magician shows the father, looking for his long-lost son who has become an actor,

---

[1] The word *comédie* was used in a variety of senses in seventeenth-century French. In addition to having the modern meaning of a light and amusing play it could stand for 1. any sort of play, including a tragedy; hence Mme de Sévigné could write: 'Racine a fait une comédie qui s'appelle *Bajazet*'; 2. a theatre, hence 'aller à la comédie' and the 'Comédie Française' (as opposed to the Théâtre Italien); 3. the art of the theatre. *Comédien* still has the meaning of an actor in any sort of play, not just a comedian.

[2] These were all actors chosen by their colleagues.

[3] *Le Théâtre français*, p.113.

[4] *L'Illusion comique* is only one of the plays of the period in which actors are depicted on the stage. Shortly before its appearance the actors of the Hôtel de Bourgogne had been portrayed in *La Comédie des comédiens* by an obscure writer named Gougenot, while those of the Théâtre du Marais appeared in Georges de Scudéry's play with the same title. In the 1650s the actors of the second of these theatres were again portrayed in Quinault's *La Comédie sans comédie*. The most interesting of all these plays is the one-act *Impromptu de Versailles* in which Molière gives us a delightful glimpse of his company rehearsing a play.

the scene at the end of the performance of a tragedy: 'Ici on relève la toile. et tous les comédiens paraissent avec leur portier, qui comptent de l'argent sur une table, et en prennent chacun leur part.' The registers of the Comédie Française which date back to 1680 show day by day in considerable detail both the takings and expenses of the theatre, and give the *part* distributed to each full-share actor. The earliest example of as detailed a document which has been preserved is the register kept by Hubert, one of Molière's actors, for the theatrical year 1672/73. We learn from it, for example, that at a performance of *Tartuffe* on 5 July 1672—not generally a very prosperous season for theatres for obvious reasons—receipts came to 217 livres and that after expenses of 61 livres 11 sous had been deducted, each full-share actor received the modest total of 11 livres. However, takings could be much larger with a new play, and even if expenses were generally higher, the actor's share rose very considerably. Thus for the first performance of *Le Malade imaginaire* in February 1673 receipts came to 1,892 livres; after expenses of 424 livres 16 sous had been deducted, the actor's *part* came to 71 livres 14 sous.

From the 1620s onwards, once Paris had become the theatrical centre of the country, the ambition of actors in companies of strolling players touring the provinces was to secure entry to one of the Paris theatres. Chappuzeau points to the instability of many of these provincial companies (Molière's seems to have been an exception) as one reason why actors in the rest of that country should seek admission to one of the Paris theatres; another reason consequent upon the first was the pensions paid to retired members of the Paris companies:

C'est à ce grand avantage qu'aspirent les comédiens de province, et les troupes de Paris sont leurs colonnes d'Hercule, où ils bornent leurs courses et leur fortune. Cette belle condition ne se peut trouver entre eux, parce que leurs troupes, pour la plupart, changent souvent, et presque tous les carêmes. Elles ont si peu de fermeté que, dès qu'il s'en est fait une, elle parle en même temps de se désunir, et soit dans cette inconstance, soit dans le peu de moyen qu'elles ont d'avoir de beaux théâtres et des lieux commodes pour les dresser, soit enfin dans le peu d'expérience de plusieurs personnes qui n'ont pas tous les talents nécessaires, il est aisé de voir la différence qui se trouve entre les troupes fixes de Paris et les troupes ambulantes des provinces.[1]

[1] *Le Théâtre français*, p.96.

Elsewhere Chappuzeau estimates that at this period in the century there were some twelve to fifteen companies of strolling players in the provinces, and he stresses once again that the ambition of the best actors in them was to come to Paris: 'C'est dans ces troupes que se fait l'apprentissage de la comédie, c'est d'où l'on tire au besoin des acteurs et des actrices qu'on juge les plus capables pour remplir les théâtres de Paris.'[1]

In the period from the 1630s down to 1680, so long as there were two or more French companies performing in Paris, there was keen rivalry between them, at times indeed bad blood. Examples of this are to be found in the plays of Molière. When his company returned to Paris in 1658, its chief rivals were not the company at the Marais theatre which was then in decline, but the 'Grands Comédiens' at the Hôtel de Bourgogne. Molière's gibes at the Hôtel de Bourgogne throw some light on the contrast between his conception of acting, particularly in tragedy, and that of the Hôtel de Bourgogne, one company favouring a more natural style of declamation as opposed to the somewhat bombastic style of the other. Thus in the *Précieuses ridicules* when the disguised lackey, posing as the Marquis de Mascarille, tells the two *précieuses* that he has written a play, and is asked which company he intends to offer it to, he gives an answer which is intended by Molière to be ironical:

Belle demande! Aux grands comédiens. Il n'y a qu'eux qui soient capables de faire valoir les choses; les autres sont des ignorants qui récitent comme l'on parle; ils ne savent pas faire ronfler les vers, et s'arrêter au bel endroit: et le moyen de connaître où est le beau vers, si le comédien ne s'y arrête, et ne vous avertit par-là qu'il faut faire le brouhaha.[2]

Again, in the bitter controversy which followed the triumph of *L'École des femmes* Molière hit back at the attacks of the rival company by caricaturing the pompous style of acting at the Hôtel de Bourgogne in his play, *L'Impromptu de Versailles*. He does this by introducing an imaginary dialogue between a play-wright and a company of actors in which, for instance, the style of acting of Montfleury, the leading tragedian of the Hôtel de Bourgogne, is mercilessly satirized:

'—Et qui fait les rois parmi vous? Voilà un acteur qui s'en démêle parfois. —Qui? Ce jeune homme bien fait? Vous moquez-vous? Il faut un roi qui

---

[1] *Le Théâtre français*, p.134.   [2] Sc. 9.

soit gros et gras comme quatre, un roi, morbleu! qui soit entripaillé comme il faut, un roi d'une vaste circonférence, et qui puisse remplir un trône de la belle manière. La belle chose qu'un roi d'une taille galante! Voilà déjà un grand défaut; mais que je l'entende un peu réciter une douzaine de vers.' Là-dessus le comédien aurait récité, par exemple, quelques vers du roi de *Nicomède:*[1]

> *Te le dirai-je, Araspe? il m'a trop bien servi;*
> *Augmentant mon pouvoir . . .*

le plus naturellement qu'il aurait été possible. Et le poète: 'Comment? vous appelez cela réciter? C'est se railler! il faut dire les choses avec emphase. Écoutez-moi.

> *Imitant Montfleury, excellent acteur de l'Hôtel de Bourgogne.*
> *Te le dirai-je, Araspe?. . . etc.*

Voyez-vous cette posture? Remarquez bien cela. Là appuyez comme il faut le dernier vers. Voilà ce qui attire l'approbation et fait faire le brou-haha.—Mais, Monsieur, aurait répondu le comédien, il me semble qu'un roi qui s'entretient tout seul avec son capitaine des gardes parle un peu plus humainement, et ne prend guère ce ton de démoniaque.—Vous ne savez ce que c'est. Allez-vous en réciter comme vous faites, vous verrez si vous ferez faire aucun ah![2]

According to his elder son, Jean Baptiste, Racine held a different view from Molière about the way in which tragedy should be acted, which accounts for the curious way in which during its first run at the Palais Royal he removed his second tragedy, *Alexandre*, to the rival theatre at the Hôtel de Bour-gogne. 'Il n'approuvait point', he declares, 'la manière trop unie de réciter établie dans la troupe de Molière. Il voulait qu'on donnât aux vers un certain son qui, joint à la mesure et aux rimes, se distingue de la prose.'[3] In another passage he states that his father persuaded his mistress, Mlle du Parc, to leave Molière's company for the Hôtel de Bourgogne 'parce que le récitatif des comédiens de ce théâtre était plus majestueux et faisait mieux valoir les vers tragiques que les acteurs de la troupe de Molière.' Boileau apparently shared this view, holding that 'tout doit être chargé[4] sur un théâtre pour rendre les objets plus sensibles. 'Je sais bien', disait-il, 'que dans de certaines occasions il ne faut pas d'emphase, mais aussi pourquoi ces lustres? ces habits magnifiques? . . . Tout se doit sentir de la noblesse des sujets dans la copie qu'on en donne.'[5]

---

[1] A tragedy of Corneille.   [2] Sc.1.
[3] L. Vaunois, *L'Enfance et la jeunesse de Racine* (Paris, 1964), p.201.
[4] In the sense of 'exaggerated, larger than life'.
[5] *L'Enfance et la jeunesse de Racine*, p.207.

The hints offered here of the different approaches to acting of the two companies do not unfortunately take us very far in the absence of sound-recordings and films of seventeenth-century actors on the stage, but passages like these do illustrate the intense rivalry between the different companies of actors.

This rivalry came out in another way. On learning through the grape-vine that another company was proposing to put on a play on a particular subject, a rival theatre would quickly find another playwright and get him to concoct a play on the same subject to be put on at the same time as the other. This competition between rival theatres is amusingly described by Chappuzeau: 'Quand une troupe promet une pièce nouvelle, l'autre se prépare à lui en opposer une semblable, si elle la croit à peu près d'égale force; autrement il y aurait de l'imprudence à s'y hasarder. Elle la tient toute prête pour le jour qu'elle peut découvrir que l'autre doit représenter la sienne, et a de fidèles espions pour savoir tout ce qui se passe dans l'état voisin.'[1] On other occasions such competition no doubt arose out of rivalry between the playwrights themselves.

There were many instances of this kind from the 1630s onwards, but probably the three best-known examples are those in which Racine was involved. On 21 November 1670 the Hôtel de Bourgogne put on a new play by Racine, his *Bérénice*; seven days later a play on the same subject by Pierre Corneille, his *Tite et Bérénice*, received its first performance by Molière's company at the Palais Royal. Enormous quantities of ink have been expended in an effort to decide whether this encounter was mere coincidence and, if not, which playwright was first in the field; the documents permit no clear-cut answer, but obviously a mere coincidence would appear rather extraordinary. The next example is more straightforward; at the end of December 1674 or the beginning of January 1675 Racine's tragedy, *Iphigénie*, which had been given its first performance at court some months earlier, was put on at the Hôtel de Bourgogne; it was not until after the following Easter, on 24 April, that a rival tragedy by Le Clerc and Coras received its first performance at the Théâtre Guénégaud. In contrast to the triumphant success of Racine's play, this only reached five performances;

[1] *Le Théâtre français*, p. 117.

yet, poor as their tragedy was, Racine had used his influence in high places to get the performance of this rival play postponed until his *Iphigénie* had enjoyed to the full its success on the public stage. He also produced a biting epigram against the two authors:

> Sur l'Iphigénie' de Le Clerc
> Entre Le Clerc et son ami Coras,
> Tous deux auteurs rimant de compagnie,
> N'a pas longtemps sourdirent grands débats
> Sur le propos de son *Iphigénie*.
> Coras lui dit: 'La pièce est de mon cru;'
> Le Clerc répond: 'Elle est mienne et non vôtre.'
> Mais aussitôt que l'ouvrage a paru,
> Plus n'ont voulu l'avoir fait l'un ni l'autre.

The best-known example of all of such rivalries is perhaps that between Racine's *Phèdre* and Pradon's *Phèdre et Hippolyte*. On this occasion there is no question but that it was Pradon who, having got wind of Racine's plans for his tragedy, decided to write a play on the same subject. Thanks to La Grange's register we know that its first run at the Théâtre Guénégaud which began on 3 January 1677 lasted for nineteen perform-ances; as usual for the Hôtel de Bourgogne we have no precise information as to the first run of Racine's tragedy, but though he may have been disappointed by the animosity which the play aroused in certain circles, there is little reason to think that it did not enjoy a similar success at the time, and the admiration which it has continued to arouse for three hundred years hardly needs mentioning. The creation of the Comédie Française in 1680 by uniting the two rival companies of French actors put an end to this rather curious form of competition.

Already in the 1630s the financial position of the Paris actors had greatly improved, now that there were two companies permanently established in the capital. In the last scene of Corneille's play, *L'Illusion comique*, the bourgeois father is at first heart-broken to learn that his long-lost son has embarked on such a disreputable and financially uncertain profession as acting. 'Mon fils comédien!' he exclaims in horror, but he is quickly reassured by the magician in the play who explains that, now the theatre has become an entertainment favoured by the highest ranks of society and even the king, the calling has become both a respected and a lucrative one:

> Cessez de vous en plaindre. A présent le théâtre
> Est en un point si haut que chacun l'idolâtre,
> Et ce que votre temps voyait avec mépris
> Est aujourd'hui l'amour de tous les bons esprits,
> L'entretien de Paris, le souhait des provinces,
> Le divertissement le plus doux de nos princes,
> Les délices du peuple, et le plaisir des grands;
> Il tient le premier rang parmi leurs passe-temps;
> Et ceux dont nous voyons la sagesse profonde
> Par ses illustres soins conserver tout le monde,[1]
> Trouvent dans les douceurs d'un spectacle si beau
> De quoi se délasser d'un si pesant fardeau.
> Même notre grand Roi, ce foudre de la guerre,
> Dont le nom se fait craindre aux deux bouts de la terre,
> Le front ceint de lauriers, daigne bien quelqufois
> Prêter l'œil et l'oreille au Théâtre français . . .
>   D'ailleurs, si par les biens[2] on prise les personnes,
> Le théâtre est un fief dont les rentes sont bonnes;
> Et votre fils recontre en un métier si doux
> Plus d'accommodement[3] qu'il n'eût trouvé chez vous.
> Défaites-vous enfin de cette erreur commune,
> Et ne vous plaignez plus de sa bonne fortune.

Even this eulogy of the theatre and of actors does contain the admission that the belief in the immorality and impecuniosity of the members of the profession was a commonly held one.

It is in this context that we must examine the famous declaration issued in 1641 by Louis XIII, no doubt at the instigation of Cardinal Richelieu. It begins by expressing the fear that 'les comédies qui se représentent utilement pour le divertissement des peuples, ne soient quelquefois accompagnées de représentations peu honnêtes, qui laissent de mauvaises impressions sur les espirits' and orders judges to impose severe penalties on those guilty of putting on such performances. However, there is no doubt that the passage which follows was intended to counteract the low reputation which professional actors had enjoyed in the past: 'Et en cas que lesdits comédiens règlent tellement les actions du théâtre qu'elles soient du tout exemptes

---

[1] A reference to the highly placed patrons which drama now enjoyed, and in particular to Richelieu.

[2] Wealth.

[3] Greater wealth.

d'impureté, nous voulons que leur exercice,[1] qui peut innocemment divertir nos peuples de diverses occupations mauvaises, ne puisse leur être imputé à blâme, ni préjudicier à leur réputation dans le commerce public . . .[2]

By this time the social status of the Paris actors had undoubtedly risen considerably. Members of the aristocracy who were genuinely interested in the theatre and not only in the charms of the actresses consorted with them socially, and although, as with the middle-class writer, there remained a social gulf between nobleman and actor, such relations did exist, and in their role as court entertainers actors came into contact not only with great noblemen, but also with the king and other members of the royal family. In comparing the attitude towards actors in a monarchy with that in a republic Chappuzeau stresses the close relations which in the former actors enjoyed with the court: 'Enfin dans un royaume les comédiens ont à qui faire agréablement la cour; le roi, la reine, les princes, les princesses et les grands seigneurs, et c'est dans ces soins et les respects qu'ils leur rendent qu'ils apprennent à se former aux belles mœurs et à l'habitude des grandes actions qu'ils doivent représenter sur le théâtre.'[3]

Throughout the century, from the reign of Henry IV onwards, companies of actors, Italian as well as French, were called upon to entertain the court in both the Louvre and Tuileries palaces and outside the capital, not only at Saint-Germain and Versailles, but also at Fontainebleau and as far away as Chambord in the Loire valley where Molière's company gave the first performance of *Le Bourgeois Gentilhomme*. Successive kings subsidized the different Paris companies; the Troupe Royale at the Hôtel de Bourgogne received a subsidy of 12,000 livres and the Théâtre du Marais one of 6,000. On its return to Paris Molière's company was known at first as the Troupe de Monsieur, the king's brother, who promised a more modest subsidy (never paid) of 300 livres an actor; but in 1665 Louis XIV took over responsibility for the company, henceforth known as the Troupe du Roi, and provided a subsidy of 6,000 livres, later increased to 7,000.

[1] Calling.
[2] C. and F. Parfaict, *Histoire du théâtre français depuis son origine jusqu'à présent* (Amsterdam and Paris, 1735–49, 15 vols.), vol.vi, pp.131–3.
[3] *Le Théâtre français*, pp.101–2.

This subsidy was no longer paid to the company when it was combined with the actors of the Théâtre du Marais to form the Théâtre Guénégaud, but from its foundation in 1680 the Comédie Française received a royal subsidy of 12,000 livres. In this reign the Italian actors, presumably because they were recruited from further afield, did even better than the French companies as they received an annual subsidy of 15,000 livres.

Moreover, when called upon to perform at court, the different companies received lavish payments both for their performances and to cover the expenses involved in travelling to places outside the capital. For the period covered by La Grange's register and by the registers of the Comédie Française we have a considerable amount of information about the generous way they were treated on these occasions. Even if Chappuzeau is sometimes naïvely optimistic in his treatment of theatrical conditions in the Paris of his day, his picturesque account of how the actors were treated when summoned to perform at court is worth quoting:

Ils sont tenus d'aller au Louvre quand le roi les mande, et on leur fournit de carrosses autant qu'il en est besoin. Mais quand ils marchent à Saint-Germain, à Chambord, à Versailles ou en d'autres lieux, outre leur pension[1] qui court toujours, outre les carrosses, chariots et chevaux qui leur sont fournis de l'écurie, ils ont de gratification en commun mille écus par mois, chacun deux écus par jour pour leur dépense, leurs gens à proportion, et leurs logements par fourriers.[2]

Nor were their creature comforts neglected:

En représentant la comédie, il est ordonné de chez le roi à chacun des acteurs et actrices, à Paris ou ailleurs, été et hiver, trois pièces de bois, une bouteille de vin, un pain et deux bougies blanches pour le Louvre, et à Saint-Germain un flambeau pesant deux livres; ce qui leur est apporté ponctuellement par les officiers de la fruiterie,[3] sur les registres de laquelle est couchée une collation de vingt-cinq écus tous les jours que les comédiens représentent chez le roi, étant alors commensaux.

On top of this the actors and actresses could count on receiving hospitality from the courtiers:

Il faut ajouter à ces avantages qu'il n'y a guère de gens de qualité qui ne soient bien aises de régaler les comédiens qui leur ont donné quelque lieu d'estime; ils tirent du plaisir de leur conversation et savent qu'en cela ils

---

[1] The royal subsidy.

[2] Court officials responsible for the allocation of lodgings.

[3] 'Dans la maison du Roi se dit de l'office qui fournit le fruit aux tables de la maison, et la bougie et la chandelle' (*Dictionnaire de l'Académie française*, 1694).

plairont au roi, qui souhaite qu'on les traite favorablement. Aussi voit-on les comédiens s'approcher le plus qu'ils peuvent des princes et des grands seigneurs, surtout de ceux qui les entretiennent dans l'esprit du roi et qui, dans les occasions, savent les appuyer de leur crédit.[1]

Until Louis XIV lost interest in the theatre in the second half of his reign as he became increasingly pious, so far as this was possible with a man so conscious of the gulf which separated him from his subjects he was on quite familiar terms with the leading actors of his time, both French and Italian. Though Molière's company had by no means a monopoly as court entertainers in the early part of Louis's personal reign, in dedicating to him his comedy, *Les Fâcheux,* which had been given its first performance at an entertainment offered to the king, he could even claim:

Je le dois, Sire, ce succès qui a passé mon attente, non seulement à cette glorieuse approbation dont Votre Majesté honora d'abord la pièce, et qui a entraîné si hautement celle de tout le monde, mais encore à l'ordre qu'Elle me donna d'y ajouter un caractère de fâcheux, dont elle eut la bonté de m'ouvrir les idées Elle-même . . .

It should not be forgotten that the actors drew additional income from the patronage of other members of the royal family, princes of the blood, great noblemen and various of the king's ministers who paid them fairly handsomely for what were known as *visites*—private performances given either in their Paris mansions or in their châteaux around the capital.

By the second half of the century quite a number of actors, as we can tell from the inventories of their possessions when they died, were undoubtedly enjoying a prosperity beyond the wildest dreams of the members of the provincial companies which in the opening decades of the century vainly sought to secure a foothold in the capital. Not only could actors and actresses be well dressed outside the theatre, but they also possessed costumes for the various parts which they took on the stage as they had to provide their own. Chappuzeau points out that while for plays written solely for the entertainment of the court, substantial sums of money were paid by the king's orders to cover the expense involved, costumes for the public stage required a heavy outlay from the actors:

[1] *Le Théâtre français,* pp.106–7.

Il y a peu de pièces nouvelles qui ne leur coûtent de nouveaux ajustments et, le faux or ni le faux argent, qui rougissent bientôt, n'y étant point employés, un seul habit à la romaine[1] ira souvent à cinq cents écus. Ils aiment mieux user de ménage[2] en toute autre chose pour donner plus de contentement au public; et il y a tel comédien dont l'équipage[3] vaut plus de dix mille francs.[4]

The prosperity of the successful actor in the second half of the century compared with the much less affluent state of even a highly successful playwright is vividly brought out by La Bruyère in a famous sentence: 'Le comédien, couché dans son carosse, jette de la boue au visage de CORNEILLE, qui est à pied.'[5] The gulf between the earnings of actor and playwright was further increased as the century wore on by the fact that, like Shakespeare, many actors also wrote plays, sometimes in large numbers. Molière is, of course, the best-known example of a seventeenth-century actor-playwright, but they were quite numerous among his contemporaries and immediate successors. Some of these succeeded in augmenting their income from acting quite considerably by their ability to appeal to contemporary audiences even if their works, unlike those of Molière, have long ceased to be performed.

On the other hand the undoubted rise of the actor in the social scale which took place in the course of this century was matched by increased hostility on the part of the Catholic Church. The contrast between the vogue which the theatre enjoyed with audiences of the time and the official attitude of the Church towards the acting profession is well brought out in another well-known passage in *Les Caractères*:

Quelle idée plus bizarre que de se représenter une foule de chrétiens de l'un et de l'autre sexe, qui se rassemblent à certains jours dans une salle pour y applaudir à une troupe d'excommuniés,[6] qui ne le sont que par le plaisir qu'ils leur donnent, et qui est déjà payé d'avance? Il me semble qu'il faudrait ou fermer les théâtres ou prononcer moins sévèrement sur l'état des comédiens.[7]

The hostility of the Catholic Church in France towards drama and actors has its curious sides. While it paralleled the fierce

---

[1] For the meaning of this expression see below, p.73. [2] Economize.
[3] Wardrobe. [4] *Le Théâtre français*, p.111.
[5] *Les Caractères*, 'Des jugements' 17.
[6] As we shall see in a moment, this is an exaggeration; actors were not strictly speaking excommunicated.
[7] 'De quelques usages' 21.

hostility of the English puritans which led in 1642 to the closing of the London theatres, it was by no means shared by the church authorities in either Catholic Italy or Catholic Spain, as Chappuzeau points out:

Mais enfin pourquoi en la matière dont il s'agit se montrer plus délicat en France qu'en Italie et à Rome même, où l'Inquisition est en vigueur pour le soutien de la religion et des bonnes mœurs? Chacun sait que les principaux directeurs du christianisme ne font point de scrupule de fournir aux frais des opéras, d'en donner le spectacle dans leurs palais, et même des gens dévoués au service de l'Église qui ont d'excellentes voix paraissent sur les théâtres publics pour y jouer un personnage en chantant . . .

N'est-ce pas à dire assez que ce sont des comédies et ceux qui les représentent des comédiens, à qui les souverains peuvent donner des privilèges comme il leur plaît? On fait sonner bien haut en Espagne le zèle de la religion, et toutefois en Espagne on voit introduire sur les théâtres publics des personnages en habit ecclésiastique, ce qui ne serait souffert en France en quelqui manière que ce fût.[1]

Moreover, clerical hostility seems to have increased in the course of the century. Certainly St. François de Sales, in his *Introduction à la vie dévote*, published in 1608, could scarcely be said to show the same attitude to the theatre and all its works as Bossuet in his *Maximes et réflexions sur la Comédie* which appeared in 1694. St. François's remarks on the subject, addressed in the first instance to a lady of the court, are relatively mild in comparison:

Les jeux, les bals, les festins, les pompes, les comédies en leur substance ne sont nullement choses mauvaises, ains[2] indifférentes, pouvant être bien et mal exercées; toujours néanmoins ces choses-là sont dangereuses, et de s'y affectionner, cela est encore plus dangereux. Je dis donc, Philothée, qu'encore qu'il soit loisible de jouer, danser, se parer, ouïr des honnêtes comédies, banqueter, si est-ce que d'avoir affection à cela, c'est chose contraire à la dévotion et extrêmem ent nuisible et dangereuse.[3]

No doubt the hostility of certain sections of the Catholic Church in France to drama and actors increased as theatre-going became a more and more fashionable form of entertainment.

In his *Maximes et réflexions sur la Comédie* Bossuet stated the position of the Church in its most extreme form when he wrote:

---

[1] *Le Théâtre français*, pp.39–40.   [2] 'ains' = 'mais' in modern French.
[3] *Introduction à la vie dévote*, 3rd edition (Lyons, 1610), p.99.

La décision en est précise dans les rituels, la pratique en est constante: on prive des sacrements, et à la vie et à la mort, ceux qui jouent la comédie, s'ils ne renoncent à leur art; on les passe à la sainte table comme des pécheurs publics; on les exclut des ordres sacrés comme des personnes infâmes; par une suite infaillible, la sépulture ecclésiastique leur est déniée.[1]

In practice relations between actors and the Church were much less clear-cut than such a statement would suggest. Though contemporaries often speak as if they were, actors were not technically excommunicated, but from the middle of the century the rituals produced by French bishops and archbishops (including that of Paris) often added them to the list of infamous persons to whom participation in the eucharist and Christian burial must be denied by their *curé*.[2]

In practice, there seems to have been all sorts of compromises, much depending on the attitude of the individual *curé*. One has to remember that until the Revolution the registration of births, deaths, and marriages was in the hands of the Church; unless actors and actresses were prepared to live in sin and to leave the births of their children without any official record, they had to have recourse to the Church for marriages and baptisms. Although because of their calling actors were also on paper debarred from acting as godparents, nevertheless they frequently did perform this service, generally for the children of other members of their company. Indeed a good deal of our information about Molière's movements, especially during his years as a strolling player, is derived from his numerous appearances in parish registers as a godfather. Only six days before his death he acted once more in this capacity. Again, in her petition to the Archbishop of Paris for her husband's body to be allowed Christian burial, his actress widow claimed that 'M. Bernard, prêtre habitué en l'église Saint-Germain, lui a adminstré les sacrements à Pâques dernier',[3] something which ought certainly not to have happened with an actor who had not by any means renounced his infamous calling.

What in practice could cause the most difficulty was the right to Christian burial. It was, generally speaking, held that

[1] C. Urbain and E. Levesque, *L'Église et le théâtre* (Paris, 1930), pp.202-3.
[2] The subject is treated in some detail in J. Dubu, 'De quelques rituels des diocèses de France au XVIIᵉ siècle et du théâtre'. *L'Année canonique*, 1957, pp.95-124.
[3] G. Mongrédien, *Recueil des textes et des documents du XVIIᵉ siècle relatifs à Molière* (Paris, 1965, 2 vols.), vol.ii, p.441.

an actor or actress must renounce the profession before he or she could receive this treatment. For instance, when in 1685 Brécourt, an actor at the Comédie Française, was on his death-bed he was compelled by his *curé* to sign the following under-taking in the presence of two more clergymen:

En présence de M. Claude Bottu de la Barmondière, prêtre docteur en théologie de la maison de Sorbonne, curé de l'église et paroisse de Saint-Sulpice à Paris, et des témoins après nommés, Guillaume Marcoureau de Brécourt a reconnu qu'ayant ci-devant fait la profession de comédien, il y renonce entièrement et promet d'un cœur véritable et sincère de ne plus exercer ni monter sur le théâtre, quoiqu'il revînt dans une pleine et entière santé.[1]

In a letter of 1698 Racine, to whom all such worldly matters were now wholly alien, described how his one-time mistress, the great tragic actress, La Champmeslé, took up at first (she changed her mind later) a very different attitude: he speaks of ' l'obsti-nation avec laquelle cette pauvre malheureuse refuse de renoncer à la comédie, ayant déclaré, à ce qu'on m'a dit, qu'elle trouvait très glorieux pour elle de mourir comédienne'.[2]

The most famous case of the denial of Christian burial to an actor in this period is, of course, that of Molière. When he fell ill on the stage at the end of the fourth performance of his latest comedy, *Le Malade imaginaire*, and died in his house a few hours later, the *curé* of his parish refused to bury him as, although he had asked for the sacraments, the third priest to be summoned arrived just too late to administer the last rites of the Church. To the devout such a refusal seemed perfectly natural. 'Qui aime la vérité', wrote a contemporary, 'aime aussi la discipline de l'Église. Et c'est ce que Monsieur le Curé de Saint-Eustache fait voir en sa conduite par le refus qu'il a fait de donner la terre sainte à un misérable farceur qui, n'ayant songé toute sa vie qu'à faire rire le monde, n'a pas pensé que Dieu se riait à la mort des pécheurs qui attendent à le réclamer jusques à cette dernière heure.'[3] His widow had to petition the Archbishop of Paris whose decision was the fairly grudging one:

---

[1] Quoted in G. Mongrédien, *La Vie quotidienne des comédiens au temps de Molière* (Paris, 1966), p.20.
[2] Racine, *Œuvres complètes*, ed. R. Picard (Paris, 1950-2, 2 vols.), vol.ii, p.610.
[3] Quoted in G. Mongrédien, *Recueil*, vol.ii, p.477.

. . . Nous avons permis au sieur curé de Saint-Eustache de donner la sépulture ecclésiastique au corps du défunt Molière dans le cimetière de la paroisse, à condition néanmoins que ce sera sans aucune pompe et avec deux prêtres seulement, et hors des heures du jour, et qu'il ne se fera aucun service solennel pour lui ni dans ladite paroisse Saint-Eustache, ni ailleurs, même dans aucune église des réguliers et que notre présente permission sera sans préjudice aux règles du rituel de notre église, que nous voulons être observées selon leur forme et teneur.[1]

Despite what Boileau called 'ce peu de terre obtenu par prière' the funeral appears to have been attended by a large crowd.

This did not, however, prevent Bossuet some twenty years later from denouncing the actor-playwright Molière in a fiery passage in his *Maximes et réflexions sur la comédie* which, as we have seen, repeated in extreme form the Church's condemnation of the stage:

On réprouvera les discours, où ce rigoureux censeur des grands canons,[2] ce grave réformateur des mines et des expressions de nos précieuses, étale cependant au plus grand jour les avantages d'une infâme tolérance dans les maris, et sollicite les femmes à de honteuses vengeances contre leurs jaloux. Il a fait voir à notre siècle le fruit qu'on peut espérer de la morale du théâtre, qui n'attaque que le ridicule du monde, en lui laissant cependant toute sa corruption. La postérité saura peut-être la fin de ce poète comédien, qui, en jouant son *Malade imaginaire* ou son *Médecin par force*, reçut la dernière atteinte de la maladie dont il mourut peu d'heures après, et passa des plaisanteries du théâtre, parmi lesquelles il rendit presque le dernier soupir, au tribunal de celui qui dit: *Malheur à vous qui riez, car vous pleurerez.*[3]

Such hostility to the theatre was shared by many laymen; the most curious case was that of Racine in the last part of his life. We find him writing to his elder son in 1695 to warn him against attending the plays and operas which were to be given at court: 'Le Roi et toute la cour savent le scrupule que je me fais d'y aller, et auraient très méchante opinion de vous si, à l'âge que vous avez, vous aviez si peu d'égard pour moi et pour mes sentiments. Je devais, avant toutes choses, vous recommander de songer toujours à votre salut, et de ne perdre point l'amour

---

[1] Mongrédien, *Recueil*, vol.ii, p.441.

[2] 'Ornement de toile rond, fort large, et souvent orné de dentelle qu'on attache au-dessous du genou, qui pend jusqu'à la moitié de la jambe pour la couvrir' (Furetière). The reference is to *Le Misanthrope*, line 483: 'Sont-ce ses grands canons qui vous le font aimer?'

[3] Urbain and Levesque, *L'Église et le théâtre*, pp. 184–5.

que je vous ai vu pour la religion.[1]

However, as we have seen, such hostility did not prevent the Paris theatres from flourishing and their actors from rising in the social scale. Whether this meant an improvement in the moral standards and behaviour of all the members of the profession is another question. If we are to believe Chappuzeau, the actors and actresses of the 1670s were very different from those of the early part of the century as described by Tallemant des Réaux. He was certainly right to contrast the attitude of the king and court towards their profession with that of its clerical and devout opponents:

L'honnête homme est honnête homme partout, et le grand et facile accès que les comédiens ont auprès du roi et des princes et de tous les grands seigneurs qui leur font caresse doit fort les consoler de se voir moins bien dans les esprits de certaines gens, qui au fond ne connaissent ni les comédiens ni la comédie, ou qui affectent de ne les connaître pas.[2]

However, when he then goes on to head the little sections into which his book is divided 'Leur assiduité aux exercices pieux', 'Leurs aumônes', ' L'éducation de leurs enfants', and 'Leur soin à ne recevoir entre eux que des gens qui vivent bien', one feels that this glowing description of the virtues of the members of the profession could scarcely be true of all. Too many documents of the time survive for one to be able to accept his account of the actors and actresses of his day as being the whole truth.

---

[1] *Œuvres complètes,* vol.ii, p.557.   [2] *Le Théâtre français,* p.88.

11 Playwrights

The best-known and undoubtedly the most prolific playwright of the opening decades of the seventeenth century, Alexandre Hardy (he died in 1632), perhaps began his career in the 1590s as an actor. Despite the valiant efforts and exciting discoveries made by Mme Deierkauf-Holsboer,[1] he still remains a very shadowy figure. Of the seven documents unearthed by her in which his name appears only one, dating from 1611, lists him among the 'comédiens du roi', His main function appears to have been to compose plays for the company to which he was attached. His total output, going back perhaps into the 1590s, was measured by himself as well as by contemporaries in hundreds. An epitaph speaks of 'plus de cinq cents poèmes'; he himself twice claimed to have written six hundred. If one looks at the agreements which he made with two companies of actors,[2] one finds a much more modest annual output; in 1620 and again in 1627 he contracted to write a mere six plays a year. What is, however, clear from the well-preserved 1620 agreement is that the playwright's relationship with the actors was one of abject dependence; he was, in the language of the time, a mere 'poète à gages', hired to write a fixed number of plays for a given period of years, in return for a share of the net takings of the company. While five years later we find the same company paying him 150 livres for a comedy (now lost), it is clear that he was in the humiliating position of not being able to publish his own plays without the actors' consent and that such consent was rarely given.[3] Hence the small proportion of his total output of plays which has come down to us.

There is some evidence that the outstanding poet of the period around 1620—the *libertin*, Théophile de Viau—also began his

---

[1] S.W. Deierkauf-Holsboer, *Vie d'Alexandre Hardy, poète du roi, 1572–1632*, New edition (Paris, 1972).

[2] pp.213–16.   [3] pp.211–12.

career as a mere *poète à gages*.[1] What is certain is that Jean
Rotrou, one of the younger generation of playwrights who
appeared on the scene around 1630 at the same time as Pierre
Corneille, began his career in a similar state of dependence and
was also unable to publish his plays without the actors' permission. This is shown by the fact that in the years 1636 and
1637 when he had been freed from what a contemporary had
earlier described as 'une servitude si honteuse',[2] he suddenly
signed agreements for the publication of as many as fourteen
plays.

By the second half of the sixteenth century thanks to the
gradual expansion of the printing industry it had become
possible for authors of literary works to receive at least modest
payments from their publishers. Even in the opening decades of
the seventeenth century the amounts received from this source
would appear to have been small. It must be remembered that
even later in the century short works like plays did not bring in
much money as sales were not large. In the 1660s, by which
time the drama had achieved a high prestige in the literary
world, one writer pointed this out in clear and unambiguous
terms: 'Une pièce peut être bonne pour les comédiens, et ne
valoir rien pour les libraires. Quand elle sort du théâtre, pour
aller au Palais, elle est presque tout usée, et la curiosité n'y fait
plus courir.[3]

Before 1630 the playwright's receipts from the publication
of his works would appear to have been extremely modest if
we may judge by the example of Alexandre Hardy who in 1625
obtained a total of a mere 180 livres from a publisher for no
fewer than twelve of his plays.[4] By the 1630s, however—a
period for which we have accidentally a good deal of information—things seem to have improved considerably. In 1630
André Mareschal did rather better than Hardy; he received 125
livres for the two *journées* of his tragi-comedy, *La Généreuse
Allemande*.[5] In 1636 Benserade did even better with 150 livres

[1] A. Adam, *Théophile de Viau et la libre pensée française en 1620*, (Paris, 1935),
pp.25-6.
[2] J. Chapelain, *Lettres*, ed. P. Tamizey de Larroque, (Paris, 1880, 2 vols.), vol.i, p.6.
[3] G. Guéret, *La Promenade de Saint-Cloud*, in F. Bruys, *Mémoires historiques,
critiques et littéraires* (Paris, 1751, 2 vols.), vol.ii, p. 205.
[4] Deierkauf-Holsboer, *Vie d'Alexandre Hardy*, pp. 210-11.
[5] G. Monval, 'André Mareschal', *Le Moliériste*, vol.ix, pp. 208-9.

for his tragedy *Cléopâtre*[1] and La Calprenède better still with 200 for his *Mithridate*.[2] In the same year Rotrou sold four plays for the sum of 750 livres and in the following year he sold ten to the same publisher for 1,500 livres.[3]

It is unfortunate that we have no information about what Corneille earned from the publication of his plays, and that what we know about the earnings of Molière and Racine from this source is very meagre. The first edition of *Tartuffe* was published, so the title-page tells us, at the author's expense; it was quickly followed by a second edition for which, according to a contemporary source, the publisher paid 2,000 livres.[4] If it is correct, this quite exceptionally high figure could be explained by the phenomenal success of this play when Molière was at last free to perform it in public in 1669. This was certainly a larger sum than the 1,500 livres which his widow received for the seven unpublished plays—*Dom Garcie de Navarre, L'Impromptu de Versailles, Dom Juan, Mélicerte, Les Amants magnifiques, La Comtesse d'Escarbagnas*, and *Le Malade imaginaire*—which appeared in the edition of his collected works published in 1682.[5] Information about what Racine earned from the publication of his plays is even scantier. It is often said that he received 200 livres for *Andromaque*, but no reputable source is given for this statement. All that Louis Racine has to say about his father's income from the publication of his plays is that 'le produit qu'il en retira fut fort modique'. He adds that he did not accept any payment from a publisher for the two plays, *Esther* and *Athalie*, which he wrote not for the public stage, but for performance by the girls of Saint-Cyr.[6]

It is then obvious that, if a playwright was to have any chance of making a living with his pen, it had to come from the performance of his works in the theatre. It is unfortunate that the records of neither the Hôtel de Bourgogne nor the Théâtre du Marais have been preserved. On the other hand it must be considered an extraordinary piece of luck that the archives of

[1] A. Jal, *Dictionnaire critique de biographie et d'histoire*, 2nd edition (Paris 1872), p. 194.
[2] H. J. Martin, *Livre, pouvoirs et société à Paris au XVIIᵉ siècle*, (Paris, 1969), p. 426.
[3] Jal, *Dictionnaire*, p. 1087.
[4] Guéret, *La Promenade de Saint-Cloud*, in Bruys, *Mémoires*, vol.ii, p. 204.
[5] De Tralage, Recueil, Bibliothèque de l'Arsenal, MS. 6544, vol.iv, 240 verso.
[6] Jean Racine, *Œuvres complètes*, vol.i, p. 41.

the Comédie Française should today contain a collection of registers which, with the exception of one theatrical year in the eighteenth century, forms an unbroken series going right back from the present day to its foundation in 1680. What is more, it also preserves the precious register kept by La Grange, one of Molière's actors; begun in 1659, this covers the activities both of Molière's company and of that of the Théâtre Guénégaud, formed after his death, and indeed continues down to 1685, over lapping with the more detailed registers of the Comédie Française.[1]

Even so, there are unfortunately enormous gaps in our information, not only about what playwrights earned from the performance of their works, but also the degree of success which these enjoyed, both during their first run and later on, if they were revived. We know nothing about what Pierre Corneille received from the actors for the performance of his plays at the Théâtre du Marais, either during the first half of his career or on the later occasions when his works were put on in that theatre. Nor do we know anything about what he received for his plays when they were performed at the Hôtel de Bourgogne; the only information we have is that in the 1660s, when he was, of course, an established author, Molière paid him 2,000 livres each for two none too successful plays, *Attila* and *Tite et Bérénice*.[2]

Racine's first tragedy, *La Thébaïde,* was also performed in the same theatre, and we know that its first run of fourteen performances brought him the modest sum of 348 livres, though this result could be regarded as fairly encouraging for a beginner.[3] Molière paid him nothing for the performances which his company gave of his second tragedy, *Alexandre le Grand*, as without saying a word to him, Racine transferred it to the Hôtel de Bourgogne whose actors were generally held to be more expert in the performance of tragedies. What he received from this theatre either for this tragedy or for all his later plays

---

[1] Further information about the activities of Molière's company can be derived from registers for certain years kept by other actors. Of these the most useful is the *Registre d'Hubert* covering the theatrical year 1672/73. This is now available in facsimile with an excellent *étude critique* by Mme S. Chevalley in the *Revue d'histoire du théâtre,* vol. xxv (1973), pp. 1-195.

[2] *Le Registre de La Grange,* vol. i, pp. 88, 118.   [3] Ibid., pp. 68-9.

from *Andromaque* to *Phèdre* we have no means of telling.

For the period between 1630 and 1659, when La Grange began to keep his register of the activities of Molière's company we are compelled to rely on one or two scraps of information and some vague hints in contemporary documents about what writers could earn from the performance of their plays. It has to be remembered that by the custom of the time once a play was published, both the actors who had first put it on and any other company were free to perform it without paying the author a penny. Moreover the idea of actually making money with one's pen, whether from publishers or—now that this had become possible through the emergence of companies of professional actors—from the théâtre, was still a new one. It is true that then as nowadays there were writers who had private means or else a job which allowed them leisure to write; Corneille held legal posts in his native Rouen for the first twenty years of his career as a playwright. For them the problem was less pressing than for those writers who had no other means of support.

Already early in his career, in the 1630s, Corneille had a reputation for striking a hard bargain with actors and publishers. In 1637 one of his rivals, Jean Mairet, wrote scornfully in one of the numerous pamphlets produced in the course of the controversy aroused by the success of *Le Cid*:

Vos caravanes de Rouen à Paris me font souvenir de ces premiers marchands qui passèrent dans les Indes; d'où par le bonheur des temps autant que par la simplicité de quelques peuples ils apportèrent de l'or, des pierreries et d'autres solides richesses, pour des sonnettes, des miroirs et de la quincaille qu'ils y laissèrent. Vous nous avez autrefois apporté la *Mélite*, la *Veuve*, la *Suivante*, la *Galerie du Palais* et de fraîche mémoire le *Cid*, qui d'abord vous a valu l'argent et la noblesse, qui vous en restent avec ce grand tintamarre de réputation qui vous bruirait encore aux oreilles, sans vos vanités et le malheur de l'impression.[1]

One has the impression that already by the 1630s and 1640s the playwrights of Corneille's generation, if and when their plays met with success on the stage, were beginning to receive fairly substantial sums of money from the theatre; more than this cannot be said since we lack any detailed information as to their earnings. While, as in this country from the Elizabethan

---

[1] 'Épître familière' in A. Gasté, *La Querelle du 'Cid'* (Paris, 1898), p. 290.

period onwards, the emergence of a professional theatre was in the long run to furnish writers with an additional source of income and thus gradually to make them less dependent on patronage than they had been in previous centuries, this was an extremely gradual process. Most playwrights of the middle decades of the seventeenth century, including Corneille, sought support from wealthy tax-farmers, great noblemen, the king's ministers, and the king himself.

The new generation of playwrights who around 1630 took over from Alexandre Hardy could almost be said to have adopted play-writing as a profession since a considerable number of them produced quite a succession of plays and not merely one or two isolated works. This was undoubtedly due not only to the greater rewards offered by the actors, but also to the existence of a variety of patrons now that theatre-going had become a much more fashionable form of entertainment.

Louis XIII would appear to have shown an interest in the theatre from his early childhood, but, if that scandalous chronicler, Tallement des Réaux, is to be believed, compared with such an enthusiastic supporter of the drama as Cardinal Richelieu, he could scarcely be described as a generous patron in his reception of the offer of the dedication of Corneille's *Polyeucte*:

Depuis la mort du Cardinal, M. de Schomberg lui dit que Corneille voulait lui dédier la tragédie de *Polyeucte*. Cela lui fit bien peur, parce que Montauron avait donné deux cents pistoles à Corneille pour *Cinna*. 'Il n'est pas nécessaire, dit-il. —Ah! Sire, reprit M. de Schomberg, ce n'est point par intérêt. —Bien donc, dit-il, il me fera plaisir.' Ce fut à la reine qu'on la dédia, car le roi mourut entre deux.[1]

The queen who received this dedication was Louis XIII's widow, Anne of Austria, who assumed power as Regent in 1643; this was by no means the only play dedicated to her as she was a fairly generous patron of men of letters. The Montauron to whom Corneille dedicated his *Cinna* in terms which scandalized even his contemporaries who were accustomed to the extravagant praise offered to patrons, was a wealthy tax-farmer who liked to splash money around. Corneille certainly laid it on thick when he wrote:

Vous avez des richesses, mais vous savez en jouir, et vous en jouissez d'une

---

[1] *Historiettes*, vol.ii, pp. 159-60.

façon si noble, si relevée, et tellement illustre, que vous forcez la voix publique d'avouer que la fortune a consulté la raison quand elle a répandu ses faveurs sur vous, et qu'on a plus de sujet de vous en souhaiter le redoublement que de vous en envier l'abondance.

Then comes the famous comparison between Montauron and the emperor Augustus:

Je dirai seulement un mot de ce que vous avez particulièrement de commun avec Auguste: c'est que cette générosité qui compose la meilleure partie de votre âme et règne sur l'autre, et qu'à juste titre on peut nommer l'âme de votre âme, puisqu'elle en fait mouvoir toutes les puissances; c'est, dis-je, que cette générosité, à l'exemple de ce grand empereur, prend plaisir à s'étendre sur les gens de lettres, en un temps où beaucoup pensent avoir trop récompensé leurs travaux quand ils les ont honorés d'une louange stérile.

Although Corneille does not actually name the sum which he expected to receive from this patron, in the last lines of the dedication he makes it perfectly clear that his dedication requires a substantial reward.

Various princes of the blood and great noblemen in this period took a considerable interest in the drama, in playwrights as well as in actresses, and proved generous patrons. Among such members of the nobility to whom Corneille dedicated his early plays were the Comte and Comtesse de Liancourt and the Duc de Longueville, the governor of Normandy. Unquestionably the most important patron of drama in the 1630s and down to his death in 1642 was Cardinal Richelieu. His interest in the theatre was no doubt responsible for the large output of new plays in these years; this was greater than in any other period of the seventeenth century.

Richelieu inspired the production of a number of plays which were performed in the Palais Cardinal which he had built for himself; these performances were attended by members of the royal family and the court. Corneille was one of the five authors who each contributed one act to a play which he commissioned, *La Comédie des Tuileries*. To the smaller theatre which he had in his palace he added in due course a larger one, later to be shared by Molière and the Italian actors. This second theatre, opened in 1641 with the performance of a spectacular tragicomedy written by one of his favourite playwrights, was technically a great advance on any of the playhouses available in

Paris down to that date. He took a considerable interest in the composition and performance of plays written by his protégés and was a generous patron of the playwrights of the period.

As can well be imagined, given the contemporary vogue for fulsome dedications, he was overwhelmed with eulogies penned by writers anxious to obtain his favours or offering thanks for those already received. All manner of works—serious and light, in prose and in verse—were dedicated to him, but plays were particularly prominent. 'N'était que Monseigneur le Cardinal se délasse parfois en l'honnête divertissement de la comédie, et que Son Éminence me fait l'honneur de me gratifier de ses bienfaits,' wrote Tristan l'Hermite in 1639 in the preface to his tragedy, *Panthée*, ' j'appliquerais peu mon loisir sur les ouvrages de théâtre.' All that even a successful play brought its author was, he declared, 'du bruit et de la fumée'. Corneille joined in the chorus of praise. If he was hurt by the way in which Richelieu had insisted on referring his *Cid* to the judgement of the newly founded Académie Française, none the less he dedicated his play to the Cardinal's favourite niece, the Duchesse d'Aiguillon. His next play, *Horace*, was dedicated to Richelieu himself. Here he begins by declaring that 'après tant de bienfaits que j'ai reçus d'elle, le silence où mon respect m'a retenu jusqu'à présent passerait pour ingratitude', and continues to the bitter end in the same grovelling tone.

Richelieu's death was undoubtedly a severe blow to the writers of the time, and particularly to the playwrights. They above all people must have echoed the sentiments expressed so irreverently in Benserade's famous epigram:

> Ci-gît, oui gît par la morbleu
> Le Cardinal de Richelieu,
> Et ce qui cause mon ennui,
> Ma pension avecque lui.[1]

The considerable decline in the number of new plays produced in the years after his death was no doubt due in the main to the failure of any new patron to take the same interest in drama; quite a number of playwrights of Corneille's generation ceased writing for the stage between Richelieu's death in 1642 and the outbreak of the Fronde in 1648. Scarron's *Épître chagrine*,

[1] *Œuvres* (Paris, 1697, 2 vols.), vol. i, p. x.

written in 1652, vividly portrays the havoc created in the literary world by Richelieu's death:

> Les pauvres courtisans des Muses
> Sont aujourd'hui traités de buses,
> Qu'autrefois défunt Richelieu,
> Qu'ils ont traité de demi-dieu,
> Traitait de la façon qu'Auguste,
> Prince aussi généreux que juste,
> A traité les hommes savants,
> Dont les vers sont encor vivants . . .
> Les beaux vers et la belle prose
> Valent aujourd'hui peu de chose:
> Se voir en auteur érigé
> Est un sinistre préjugé
> Pour la fortune d'un pauvre homme.[1]

Scarron does, however, mention the existence of at least one patron in high office—Pierre Séguier, who was Chancellor from 1635 to 1672 and who succeeded Richelieu as patron of the Académie Française. Somewhat cynically Tallemant wrote of his favours to men of letters: 'Pour être loué, il donnait sur le sceau, et à proprement parler, c'était le public qui payait ces beaux esprits.'[2] Séguier duly received his quota of dedicatory epistles; as well as getting one from Scarron, he found himself addressed by Corneille in the usual flowery terms in the dedication to his tragedy, *Héraclius* (1647):

. . . Les nouvelles faveurs que j'ai reçues de vous m'ont donné une juste impatience de les publier; et les applaudissements qui ont suivi les représentations de ce poème m'ont fait présumer que sa bonne fortune pourrait suppléer à son peu de mérite . . . On sait par toute l'Europe l'accueil favorable que Votre Grandeur fait aux gens de lettres . . . Votre bonté ne dédaigne pas de répandre sur moi votre bienveillance et vos grâces.

Scarron, however, does leave out a literary patron of some importance, Cardinal Mazarin, Richelieu's successor as prime minister. This was no doubt because Scarron had received no financial reward when he dedicated one of his works to him.

Certainly Mazarin was not so exceptionally generous a patron of men of letters as Richelieu had been, but when his unpopularity during the Fronde led to frequent attacks on his failure

---

[1] *Poésies diverses*, ed. M. Cauchie (Paris, 1947-61, 2 vols.), vol. ii, pp. 57-8.
[2] *Historiettes*, vol. iii, p. 131.

to assist writers, his librarian produced a long list of authors who had not only received from him various pensions and gifts, but had also rained eulogies upon him. He quoted, for instance, the poem in which Corneille had offered thanks for the pension of 2,000 livres which Mazarin had given him for the dedication of his tragedy, *Pompée:*

> C'est toi, grand cardinal, âme au-dessus de l'homme,
> Rare don qu'à la France ont fait le ciel et Rome . . .[1]

After the collapse of the Fronde in 1653 dedicatory epistles once more rained down on Mazarin, amongst others from playwrights such as Pierre Corneille's younger brother, Thomas, and another rising dramatist, Philippe Quinault. These frequently earned pensions and other favours; what is more, in his will, made in March 1661 just before his death, Mazarin took care to ensure that the pensions were paid throughout the lifetime of the recipients and did not die with him.

None the less it is clear that in his last years Mazarin was eclipsed as a patron by another member of the government, Nicolas Foucquet, the Surintendant des Finances; in the eight years in which he held this office until his downfall in 1661 he gradually built up for himself a considerable clientèle among the writers of the period. Foucquet counted La Fontaine among his numerous protégés, and it was he who induced Pierre Corneille, who had given up writing for the stage in 1651, to return in 1659 with his tragedy, *Œdipe*, and to embark on a second career of play-writing which was to last until 1674 and thus overlap with that of the much younger Racine, born a whole generation later. The first edition of *Œdipe* opens with a poem addressed to Foucquet which contains the lines:

> Oui, généreux appui de tout notre Parnasse,
> Tu me rends ma vigueur lorsque tu me fais grâce . . .[2]
> Je sens le même feu, je sens la même audace,
> Qui fit plaindre le Cid, qui fit combattre Horace;
> Et je me trouve encor la main qui crayonna
> L'âme du grand Pompée et l'esprit de Cinna.

Corneille received his reward of 2,000 livres in hard cash, though

---

[1] *Œuvres complètes*, ed. C. Marty-Laveaux (Paris, 1868, 12 vols.), vol. x, p. 95.
[2] i.e. 'confer favours upon me'.

whether this was a once-for-all gift or a pension remains unclear.

The preface to *Œdipe* also mentions another source of patronage which Corneille was fortunate enough to tap; the twenty-year-old Louis XIV who was present along with the court at the first performance of the play at the Hôtel de Bourgogne, gave him what he describes in his *Au lecteur* as 'de véritables et solides marques de son approbation'.

Though from the beginning of his personal reign two years later Louis XIV was to be the outstanding patron of men of letters, this does not mean that other sources of support had entirely dried up. It is true that it became less common to dedicate plays to patrons; the poem addressed to Foucquet was to be Corneille's last dedicatory epistle, and both Molière and Racine gave up penning the usual fulsome eulogies once their reputation was solidly established. Yet princes of the blood and great noblemen continued to act as patrons to playwrights as well as to other men of letters. For instance, when Pierre Corneille at last moved permanently from Rouen to Paris in 1662, he and his family appear to have been accomodated for some time in the mansion of the Duc de Guise. One particularly prominent patron, over a period extending from the 1640s to the 1680s, was the Comte, later Duc, de Saint-Aignan, *de l'Académie française*. Racine dedicated his first tragedy to him, and the writers who offered their plays to him ranged from Tristan l'Hermite in 1645 to Boursault in 1683. Boursault was one of those who was rewarded with hard cash, as he himself relates:

Par reconnaissance de la protection qu'il m'avait donnée, je lui dédiai *Marie Stuart*, une tragédie que j'avais faite. Il la reçut de la manière la plus obligeante . . . et me pria de ne pas trouver mauvais que pour s'acquitter faiblement de l'obligation qu'il m'avait, il me fît un présent de cent louis.

As Boursault hesitated to accept such a large sum from a not very affluent nobleman,

'Je vois bien, ajouta-t-il, que vous ne me croyez pas assez riche pour vous donner cent louis tout d'un coup. Eh bien, puisque vous voulez avoir la complaisance de vous accommoder à ma fortune, souffrez au moins que je vous en donne vingt présentement, et que je continue de mois en mois jusqu'à ce que j'en sois quitte.'

Boursault assures the reader that the instalments were promptly paid.[1]

A striking example of a great nobleman's patronage of a playwright a few years later is furnished by the Duc de Vendôme's bounty to Racine's successor in tragedy, Campistron, who is chiefly remembered today for Hugo's line:

Sur le Racine mort le Campistron pullule.

In 1691 he wrote the libretto for an opera for a performance at a fête held at the duke's château at Anet. According to the brothers Parfaict, the eighteenth-century historians of the French theatre, the duke was so pleased with it that he sent the author 100 louis. However, his friends assured him that 'la somme n'était pas assez pour M. de Vendôme et qu'il pouvait en espérer une récompense plus considérable'.[2] Campistron was only with difficulty persuaded to refuse the money, but he found in the end that he had done well to follow their advice. The duke took him into his household and made him *secrétaire de ses commandements* and in 1694 he secured for him the post of *secrétaire général des galères* which carried with it a salary of 3,000 livres.[3]

Unquestionably all other patrons of men of letters were eclipsed by Louis XIV when he renewed the tradition of literary patronage of the Valois kings in the sixteenth century by his much publicized grant of pensions to men of letters, scholars, and scientists, foreign as well as French. It was in 1663 that the first of these payments were made by Colbert as Surintendant des Bâtiments, acting on the advice of the poet and critic, Chapelain. One must not, however, allow oneself to be taken in by the publicity which in the 1660s surrounded these gifts to men of letters; not only was the total amount distributed never very large, but with the growing cost of wars and the court they gradually tended to be paid less regularly. Some went to playwrights—not only to Pierre Corneille, Molière, and later Racine, but also to Thomas Corneille, Quinault, and some now forgotten writers—but after 1673 Pierre Corneille received nothing for nine years, until shortly before his death in 1684. Even before

---

[1] *Lettres nouvelles* (Paris, 1722, 3 vols.), vol. i, p. 129.
[2] C. and F. Parfaict, *Histoire du théâtre français*, vol. xiii, p. 231.
[3] Jal, *Dictionnaire*, p. 309.

that, like many other people, he had suffered delays in the payment of his pension, a situation which produced the following
lines which are generally attributed to him:

Au Roi, sur le retardement du paiement de sa pension.

> Grand Roi, dont nous voyons la générosité
> Montrer pour le Parnasse un excès de bonté
> Que n'ont jamais eu tous les autres,
> Puissiez-vous dans cent ans donner encore des lois,
> Et puissent tous vos ans être de quinze mois
> Comme vos commis font les nôtres.

Though the chaotic state of the Treasury accounts makes it
difficult to know exactly when these royal gifts to men of
letters faded out, they do not seem, even on this restricted
scale, to have lasted beyond 1690.

In the years in which he received these gifts, Pierre Corneille
was understandably treated better than any other playwright
with a grant of 2,000 livres. Molière as an actor received a share
in the royal subsidy paid to his company; as a man of letters he
had to be content with gifts of 1,000 livres. Racine began as a
poet with a modest 600 livres in 1664 at a time when he had
yet to make a reputation as a playwright; by 1668, after the
success of *Andromaque*, this had been raised to 1,200 and by
1670 to 1,500 livres; by 1679, by which time he had given up
writing for the public stage, it had climbed to 2,000.

Whenever one endeavours to investigate in detail the workings
of literary patronage under the Ancien Régime, one invariably
comes across all sorts of loose ends. If Louis XIV's interest in
literature in general and particularly in the theatre, gradually
waned, he could confer gifts and favours on playwrights which
are not listed in the accounts of Colbert's ministry. For instance,
while Racine was still active as a playwright, in 1674—the year
of the triumphant success of his *Iphigénie*—the king made him a
present of the official post of *trésorier de France*, a sinecure
which brought in an income of 2,400 livres a year and which
was valued at 36,000 livres in his marriage contract three years
later.

Patronage thus continued in the second half of the century
to make an important contribution to the income of the playwrights of the period. Yet, although what they received from

the publication of their plays seems to have remained modest, by this time receipts from their performance in the theatre could reach quite large figures and must undoubtedly have been much greater than in the 1630s when the theatre was just beginning to be a fashionable entertainment. If our information still remains exactly nil for the Hôtel de Bourgogne, we have La Grange's register for the period from 1659 onwards and from 1680 those of the Comédie Française.

In La Grange's register we still find some established playwrights being paid a lump sum for the performance of their works; such was the case with the two plays which Pierre Corneille had put on in Molière's theatre. However, a new sysstem of payment had come in by the 1660s and soon became universally accepted; under it the actors paid the author for each performance of his play a share of the net receipts after deduction of all expenses. For a five-act play the author received two shares and proportionately less for shorter works. If the play was a failure and had to be taken off after only a small number of performances, the author received very little; but if the play was a success, he could earn quite a large sum of money.

It is unfortunate that we are entirely without information as to what Racine earned from the performance of his plays beyond the relatively modest sum (348 livres) which his first tragedy, *La Thébaïde*, brought him in Molière's theatre. Although he had his ups and downs in his career as a playwright, *Andromaque* scored a considerable success and must have had quite a long first run. If both his only comedy, *Les Plaideurs*, and *Britannicus* appear to have been coolly received when first put on, he could claim in the preface to *Bérénice* that 'la trentième représentation a été aussi suivie que la première', a very successful first run by the standards of the time. *Bajazet* and *Mithridate* both appear to have scored an immediate success, while *Iphigénie* was probably the Racine tragedy which had the longest first run since a contemporary declares that this lasted for forty performances, a quite exceptional triumph in any Paris theatre of the period. Although Racine was disgusted at the success enjoyed by the play of his rival, Pradon, there is no evidence to show that his *Phèdre* did not have a fairly long first run.

The performance of his nine tragedies and one comedy must

have earned him a fairly substantial sum of money in the thir-
teen years between 1664 and 1677, perhaps at least 15,000
livres. It is possible to make some comparisons with other playwrights whose careers overlap with his or come slightly later
and for whom we have quite precise information in theatrical
records. For six tragedies performed between 1674 and 1697
Pradon received from the actors just under 7,000 livres, an
average of a little over 1,000 livres a play. A better comparison
is with the career of Campistron; he wrote the same number of
plays as Racine in a roughly similar period of years. Between
1683 and 1693 he produced an average of one play a year with
his nine tragedies and one comedy. While some of his plays (his
Alcibiade for instance) were highly lucrative by the standards of
the time, two of his tragedies had so little success that they
were never published, while his comedy was not printed until
1715. The total sum which he received for these ten plays was
in the neighbourhood of 11,500 livres, or again just over 1,000
a year. No doubt Racine did rather better than this with his ten
plays.

In the closing decades of the seventeenth century writers
could earn relatively large sums of money during the first run
of their plays. The record, so far as professional writers were
concerned, was held by Thomas Corneille and Donneau de Visé
with their *pièce à machines, La Devineresse*, for which they
shared 5,651 livres. The most lucrative tragedy was Campistron's
Alcibiade which brought him 2,839 livres, and in comedy the
highest figure was achieved by Boursault with *Les Fables d'Ésope*
for which he received 3,291 livres from the actors.

The example of Boursault, a minor but at times successful
playwright, whose most important works were performed after
Racine's abandonment of the public theatre, is an interesting
one. Between 1683 and 1694 he had five plays produced at the
Comédie Française:

1683.   *Le Mercure Galant*, comedy, 5 acts: 18 performances: 1,527 livres.
        Marie Stuart, tragedy: 7 performances: 228 livres 4 sous.
1690.   *Les Fables d'Ésope*, comedy, 5 acts: 43 performances: 3,291 livres.
1691.   *Phaëton*, comedy, 5 acts: 9 performances: no payment because of
        the heavy expenses in which the production of the play involved
        the actors.

1694. *Les Mots à la mode*, comedy, 1 act: 19 performances: 328 livres
10 sous.

Thus over a period of eleven years Boursault received from the
actors the sum of just over 5,000 livres for one tragedy, three
full-length comedies, and a one-act play. Yet two of his five-
act comedies were highly successful, his *Fables d'Ésope* bringing
in a record sum for the first two decades in the life of
the Comédie Française.

In a letter to his wife during the successful first run of his
Ésope, Boursault has a very illuminating comment to make on
the economic position of playwrights in this period. This letter
is especially interesting as it is one of the rare documents of the
time in which one finds a playwright discussing such bread-and-
butter questions. 'Il n'y a que cinq pistoles [= 50 livres]à dire',
he writes, 'que mes deux parts ne montent déjà à mille écus
[= 3,000 livres]; et si le carême eût été une fois plus long, je suis
sûr qu'elles auraient monté à plus de cinq cents. A vue de pays,
elles iront à près de quatre mille livres, sans l'impression.'[1] If we
have seen this forecast to have been over-optimistic (Boursault
was some 700 livres out in his calculations), his concluding
remark on this subject might be said to contain the key to the
whole question of the adequacy of the financial rewards offered
to French playwrights in the second half of the century: 'Qui
serait assuré de faire deux pièces par an avec le même succès,
n'aurait guère besoin d'autre emploi.'[2]

In common with all the other playwrights of the age Boursault was obviously unable to achieve two successes of this kind
in a year. His *Lettres nouvelles* contains various references to his
impecuniosity and that of his fellow-playwrights, as, for instance,
in the following lines:

> Un auteur du théâtre, expert, mais indigent,
>   (Cela n'est pas une merveille),
> Allait un jour, faute d'argent,
>   Vendre les ouvrages de Corneille;
> Un ami qui le vit inquiet et rêveur:
>   Quel chagrin, lui dit-il, me faites-vous paraître?
> On en aurait à moins, lui répondit l'auteur;
>   Je ressemble à Judas; je vais vendre mon maître.[3]

---

[1] *Lettres nouvelles*, vol. i, p. 258.   [2] Ibid., vol. ii, p. 186.   [3] Ibid., vol. i, p. 129.

Indeed, far from producing two successful plays a year, he had two failures among the five plays which he produced in the space of eleven years. It was only by the happy accident of finding an aristocratic patron in the Duc de Saint-Aignan to whom he dedicated his *Marie Stuart* that he managed to get anything more than pocket-money out of his tragedy. It is true that the risk of writing an unsuccessful play is at least as great today as it was in seventeenth-century France, even though the play in question may later be acclaimed as a masterpiece. It is no reflection on the actors of the time that they were unable to provide large rewards for plays which did not find favour with audiences, though these were to survive their first failure. But it remains an undoubted fact that, even in the case of successful plays, the rewards offered to their writers were inadequate.

The real trouble was that, down to the eve of the Revolution, the profits derived by a playwright from the performance of his works were limited to those which were made from their first run. As, judged by modern standards, this first run was always a short one, his earnings were inevitably meagre. Once his play was published (generally as soon as this first run was over and he could hope for nothing more from the actors) it was open to anyone, in Paris or the provinces, to perform it without payment. Even the company which had originally put on his play was now free to exploit it without offering him another penny.

It is often assumed that this failure to continue payments to authors beyond the first run of their plays was due to mere cupidity on the part of the actors, and also that, given a continued share in the receipts from all later performances of their work, the playwrights of seventeenth-century France would have been in a much better financial position. There is obviously some truth in both these contentions; yet an examination of the registers of the Comédie Française from 1680 onwards leads one to modify this interpretation of the facts. It is, for instance, true that Racine's plays were very frequently performed at the Comédie Française between 1680 and his death in 1699 and that he was not thereby a penny better off. The fault did not, however, lie wholly with the actors. The total number of performances of his plays, as of those of Corneille and Molière, given there was certainly very impressive; but it is also important to know how many spectators these performances attracted and what was the actors' reward from them.

If we examine the records of the first year's workings of the Comédie Française, from August 1680 to August 1681, we find that, including six performances of *Les Plaideurs*, altogether forty-nine performances of plays of Racine were given. The first of these was *Phèdre* which attracted 1,045 paying spectators and produced receipts of 1,424 livres. That, however, was the opening performance of the newly founded Comédie Française, and the receipts were exceptionally good. Taking the year as a whole, we find that on twenty-nine occasions out of forty-nine a Racine play failed to attract as many as 400 paying spectators. On two occasions less than 150 (145 and 123) were present; this meant that the individual actor's share of the receipts was only 5 livres 10 sous and 1 livre 10 sous respectively—earnings which could scarcely be described as profiteering.

Ten years later, in the theatrical year 1690–91, thirty-one performances of plays by Racine were given, including three of *Les Plaideurs*. This time there was not one outstandingly re-munerative performance; indeed at twenty-one out of thirty-one performances the attendance fell below 400 paying spectators. Two performances, those of *La Thébaïde* and *Alexandre,* brought the actors precisely nothing. It is perhaps scarcely sur-prising that a revival of his first two tragedies should have failed to attract much of an audience, but it is surely significant that the actor's earnings for the day were thrice reduced to the mod-est figure of 1 livre 11 sous by performances of such undoubted masterpieces as *Iphigénie, Bérénice,* and *Mithridate.*

For the last year of Racine's life (22 April 1698–21 April 1699) the results were rather better as the ending of the Nine Years War in 1697 had brought more prosperous times to the Comédie Française. In September 1698 a performance of *Bajazet* attracted 1,196 paying spectators and produced receipts of 1,635 livres, which meant that each full-share actor received nearly 60 livres. A performance of *Britannicus* in November also attracted over a thousand paying spectators and gave the actors nearly 47 livres each. In addition, there were a number of fairly profitable performances at various times in this year; yet, even so, at eight out of a total of thirty-seven performances less than

400 paying spectators were attracted to the theatre to see a
Racine play. One performance of *Mithridate* and two of *Les
Plaideurs* brought no return whatsoever to the actors.

The conclusion which one may draw from a study of the
registers of the Comédie Française is that the failure of the Paris
theatres to offer a steady income even to a successful playwright
like Racine was not wholly due to the avarice of the actors.
While certain plays continued to be frequently revived as a
regular part of the repertoire of the Comédie Française, they
sometimes failed to bring any financial reward even to the actors.
Though a revival might occasionally attract large audiences, the
playwright, had he been permitted to enjoy a share of the proceeds, would not have profited greatly from such more or less
isolated performances. The fact is that, judged by modern standards, only a short run could be enjoyed by the most successful
play; and, if it was revived, its success was uncertain and inter-
mittent because, generally speaking, large audiences could be
expected only at the height of the season, in winter, or when
new plays were put on.

The responsibility for this unfortunate state of affairs lay,
not with the actors, but with the smallness of the theatre-going
public in seventeenth-century Paris.[1]

If we return to La Bruyère's picture of the haughty actor in
his carriage and Corneille on foot, we find that there was in fact
a marked contrast between the earnings of the two partners in
any theatrical performance. Whereas those of the playwright
were sporadic and confined to the first run of each new play,
the actor's income was fairly regular and reasonably assured,
and he could also count on a pension of 1,000 livres a year
when he retired. We learn from La Grange's register that the
earnings of a full-share actor in Molière's company from Easter
1659 to Easter 1673 came to a total of 51,670 livres 14 sous—
an average of over 3,500 livres a year.[2] Leaving aside his share
in the royal subsidy (some 1,000 livres a year), the full-share
actor at the Comédie Française in the period 1680–1701 enjoyed
an income varying between 2,803 livres in 1693–94 and 7,159
livres in 1698–99. His average earnings for the period, again without his share in the royal subsidy, were in the neighbourhood of

---

[1] See Chapter IV.   [2] Vol. i, p. 145.

4,900 livres. The contrast with the fortunes of a prolific writer like Campistron, whose ten plays in ten years produced an average yearly income of just over 1,000 livres, is striking.

This disproportion between the earnings of actor and playwright is brought out even more forcibly if we compare the average earnings of the *individual full-share actor* with the total amount paid to *all authors of new plays* in any given year. If we take the average at the Comédie Française for the twenty complete years from Easter 1681 to Easter 1701, we find that the amount paid out each year to *all* authors of new plays works out at a little over 5,300 livres—less than *each* full-share actor earned in an average year when he had received his share of the royal subsidy.

Moreover, we must not forget that a considerable share of the money paid out to authors went to actor-playwrights. Although the yawning gaps in our information about the finances of the different Paris theatres for the whole of the century make it unwise to pronounce dogmatically on the point, it is fairly certain that the best-paid playwright of the century was Molière. On top of average earnings as an actor during the period from 1658 to 1673 of over 3,000 livres (from 1662 onwards his wife also earned on the same scale), on top of the royal pension of 1,000 livres which he received as a man of letters, he drew an estimated total of 50,000 livres from the performance of his plays. The tradition which he had a great part in founding continued after his death, to a slight extent in tragedy, but chiefly in comedy.

In the first twenty years of its existence the Comédie Française put on a great variety of plays written by actors of the company. The most famous of these was Dancourt; between 1683 when he made his début there and 1700 he had over thirty plays performed at the Comédie Française—full-length comedies, plays in three acts and, most frequently of all, in one act. In these seventeen years, over and above his income as an actor, he earned from them some 20,000 livres fairly regularly distributed over the whole period. In fact in the period 1680-1701 not far short of 40 per cent of the sums paid out by the Comédie Française to playwrights went to Dancourt and some half a dozen other actors of the company.

Seen against this background Racine's abandonment of the

public theatre seems understandable. It is reasonably clear that it was not religious scruples, but the prospects of worldly advancement through a career at court that led him to forsake the drama after *Phèdre* for the post of *historiographe du roi* with its greater social prestige and its higher and more permanent emoluments. For Voltaire, one of his successors in this post, this seemed the obvious and natural interpretation of the facts. 'Il faut travailler jusqu'au dernier moment de sa vie', he wrote to a friend in 1752, 'et ne point imiter Racine, qui fut assez sot pour aimer mieux être un courtisan qu'un grand homme.'[1] But it was all very well for Voltaire, with a large fortune acquired outside his profession of man of letters, to add: 'Imitons Corneille, qui travailla toujours, et tâchons de faire de meilleurs ouvrages que ceux de sa vieillesse.' Racine, who actually witnessed the latter part of the career of his great rival in tragedy, can scarcely have been encouraged by such an example to continue to the bitter end as a playwright. It may be that Corneille tended to exaggerate his poverty; but it is clear that despite a reputation for avarice handed down by a dozen contemporaries, he had not succeeded in making the profession of playwright pay. A lifetime of writing for the theatre, over thirty plays, had produced for him only the most modest reward. It is true that we have no precise information as to what he earned for the vast majority of his plays, but his biographers have made it clear that he died a relatively poor man.

Under the circumstances it is not surprising that Racine, already at the sobering age of thirty-seven and recently married, should, to our great loss, have decided to abandon his art for a career at court. That he should have been persuaded to take this step shows that the patronage extended by Louis XIV to the literary men of his age was not always beneficent in its effects. Yet, however much one may be repelled by the king's inordinate fondness for flattery and worship, the causes of Racine's abandonment of the theatre go deeper. We can scarcely blame Louis for the failure of the seventeenth-century Paris theatre to provide even a successful playwright with a good living. If Racine was unable to secure adequate rewards for his plays, the cause lay,

---

[1] *Correspondence and Related Documents*, ed. T. Besterman (vols. 85-135 of *Complete Works*, Geneva, Banbury, and Oxford, 1968-77), vol. xiii, p. 11.

not in Louis XIV's vanity, but in the parsimony of the actors and even more in the failure of the society of his age to produce a large theatre-going public.

One could argue, of course, that the economic problem could have been solved if, instead of wasting Racine's talents by turning him into a pseudo-historian and hanger-on at court, Louis had been prepared to give him the same financial advantages to enable him to carry on his career as playwright. But this would be to leave out of account the social conditions and outlook of seventeenth-century France. In that aristocratic society the profession of playwright, as of man of letters in general, was still looked down upon. A typical example of the prevailing attitude of snobbish contempt shown towards playwrights is to be found in the reception offered to Racine's one-time rival, Quinault, when, after making a wealthy marriage, he bought himself a post in the Chambre des Comptes. He encountered strong opposition from his prospective colleagues who, in the words of his biographer, writing in 1715, were far from keen to receive 'dans une compagnie aussi grave que la leur, un homme qui avait paru pendant plusieurs années sur les théâtres pour y faire représenter des tragédies et des comédies'.[1] Racine's skill in adapting himself to the atmosphere of the court is reflected in the way he warned his elder son that it was not his plays which brought him flattering attentions among the princes of the blood and great noblemen in whose circles he now moved:

. . . Sans fatiguer les gens du monde du récit de mes ouvrages dont je ne leur parle jamais, je me contente de leur tenir des propos amusants, et de les entretenir de choses qui leur plaisent. Mon talent avec eux n'est pas de leur faire sentir que j'ai de l'esprit, mais de leur apprendre qu'ils en ont. Ainsi quand vous voyez M. le Duc passer souvent des heures entières avec moi, vous seriez étonné, si vous étiez présent, de voir que souvent il en sort sans que j'ai dit quatre paroles; mais peu à peu je le mets en humeur de causer et il sort de chez moi encore plus satisfait de lui que de moi.[2]

Such were the methods used by Racine to obliterate gradually the memory of his bourgeois status as a writer. Both his success in this endeavour and the aristocratic disdain for the writer are admirably reflected in the verdict passed on him in the memoirs

---

[1] *Théâtre* (Paris, 1715, 5 vols.), vol. i, p. 19.   [2] *Œuvres complètes*, vol. i, pp. 81–2.

of the Duc de Saint-Simon: 'Rien du poète dans son commerce, et tout de l'honnête homme'.[1]

It was inevitable that writers like Racine and his friend, Boileau, who shared the post of *historiographe* with him, should in their turn blush for their profession and seek entry into the higher circles of the aristocracy and the court. Even the thoroughly bourgeois Boileau could speak of his appointment as 'le glorieux emploi qui m'a tiré du métier de la poésie'.[2] A similar phrase is applied to Racine by a slightly later playwright who composed one of the many parallels between Corneille and Racine which have been perpetrated since the closing years of the seventeenth century; though he declares that everyone deplores the loss sustained by the theatre because of Racine's new role as panegyrist of the king, he exclaims: 'Heureux de pouvoir jouir lui-même des regrets du public (bonheur qui n'est pas fait pour les vivants) et de devoir à l'emploi glorieux qui l'a tiré du théâtre ce premier gage d'immortalité.'[3]

Against such a deeply rooted prejudice, widespread and tenacious as the documents of the time prove, and forced upon the writer himself by the influence of the upper classes of society, the absolutism of Louis XIV would have battled in vain. Racine's abandonment of his career as a playwright was thus due, less to Louis's blind egoism, than to the conditions which prevented him from deriving either wealth or social position from the theatre.

We may conclude then that, in the last part of the seventeenth century, the improvement in the financial rewards offered by the actors to playwrights had more or less kept pace with the progress made by the theatre since the days of Alexandre Hardy and other *poètes à gages*. On the other hand these rewards were still far from reaching the level of the nineteenth century, by which time a series of successful plays could bring wealth to a dramatist. Though the emergence of a professional theatre had provided writers with a fresh source of income, the earnings of playwrights were still not sufficient to offer a good livelihood. This state of affairs explains the apparent paradox that under

[1] *Mémoires*, ed. A. de Boislisle (Paris, 1879–1930, 43 vols.), vol. vi, p. 170.

[2] *Œuvres complètes*, ed. A. Adam (Paris, 1966), p. 857.

[3] Published in A. Baillet, *Jugements des savants* (Amsterdam, 1725, 8 vols.), vol. iv, p. 385.

the Ancien Régime the theatre attracted writers only to repel them again. A successful play brought in day by day during its first run a sum of money which must have appeared large to the impecunious author at the beginning of his career. If his luck was good, he could certainly earn more ready cash in the theatre than from any other form of writing at a time when payments from publishers, even for established authors, were very small. Even more important perhaps than the purely economic motive was the fact that, in a period when literary reputations were conferred by relatively restricted circles in Paris, the theatre was the high road to fame and renown. Through a successful play the young writer could get himself known almost overnight both in the *salons* of the capital and among a rather wider public. This point was made clear by a contemporary when he wrote:

Comme la plupart des gens du siècle ne pensent qu'à leur plaisir, ce leur est une chose fort agréable de s'entretenir des comédies qu'on représente; aussi aucun auteur n'acquiert de la réputation en si peu de temps que ceux qui ont travaillé pour le théâtre. En cinq ou six représentations de leur pièce il se trouve que quatre ou cinq mille personnes y ont assisté, et en font le rapport aux autres.[1]

Yet, though caught up in this gold-rush, the professional playwright soon discovered that the payments he received from the actors, which had at first seemed generous, were not in practice enough to provide him with a living, however prolific and successful his efforts might be. He found in the long run that while the theatre might give him a reputation, it could not provide him with a livelihood. To stay too long in the profession meant a reward no greater than that received by Pierre Gorneille and his younger brother, Thomas. A more secure and permanent income could only be found elsewhere by using the reputation which he had acquired in the theatre as a stepping-stone to more lucrative and respectable occupations. Racine's case is by no means unique. Before him Quinault had sought refuge in a wealthy marriage which enabled him in due course to purchase both a minor post at court and one in the Chambre des Comptes and gradually to abandon writing for the Paris stage and to collaborate with Lulli in the production of operas, the latest infatuation of their master, Louis XIV. After Quinault and

---

[1] Charles Sorel, *Bibliothèque française* (Paris, 1667), p. 211.

and Racine Campistron, as we have seen, abandoned writing for the stage to become the secretary of the Duc de Vendôme who secured for him a relatively well paid post in the public service.

No doubt the loss sustained in this way by French drama was seldom severe; there was not always a Racine at stake. It is, however, clear what an unsatisfactory career was offered to the professional playwright in this great age in the history of French drama. Right down to the Revolution the economic and social status of the man of letters explains both this rush of young writers to the theatre and the frequency with which they abandoned it when success and reputation, but not wealth, had been won. Indeed in France it was only in the nineteenth century, when a greatly enlarged audience and reading public brought greater financial rewards from actors and publishers, that an author could hope to make a living by writing for the stage—provided he knew how to please his public.

III Inside a theatre

The seventeenth-century Paris theatre-goer did not seek his entertainment between roughly nine o'clock in the evening and midnight. In this period performances frequently started much earlier in the day, indeed often as early as two o'clock, especially in winter. In 1619 a *règlement* of the *Lieutenant civil* forbade actors 'depuis le jour de saint Martin jusqu'au quinzième février, de jouer passé quatre heures et demie au plus tard; auxquels pour cet effet enjoignons de commencer précisément avec telles personnes qu'il y aura à deux heures après midi, et finir à ladite heure; que la porte soit ouverte à une heure précise . . .'[1] Few theatre posters of the time have survived and then often only in fragments, but a number for the period around 1660 which have come down to us also give 'deux heures' as the time that the curtain was due to go up.[2] It would seem, however, that later in the century theatrical performances began considerably later; in 1687, when the actors of the Comédie Française were compelled to seek a site for a new theatre, they addressed a petition to the *Lieutenant de police* in the course of which they state categorically: 'La comédie ne commence qu'après cinq heures.'[3] Five o'clock or even rather later was certainly the time at which most theatres began their performances in eighteenth-century Paris.

When the spectator had made his way through the muddy and smelly streets of the capital either in a carriage or, much more messily, on foot, he found himself in a building which scarcely coincided with our idea of what the inside of a theatre should look like. It was not until 1689 when the Comédie

---

[1] N. de Lamare, *Traité de la police,* vol. i, p. 440.

[2] See S. Chevalley, *Album Théâtre classique. La Vie théâtrale sous Louis XIII et Louis XIV* (Paris, 1970), pp. 69, 74, 81, 86.

[3] N. Bourdel, ' L'Établissement et la construction de l'Hôtel des Comédiens Français rue des Fossés-Saint-Germain-des-Prés (Ancienne Comédie) 1687–1690', *Revue d'histoire du théâtre,* 1955, p. 152.

Française inaugurated its new building in the Rue des Fossés-Saint-Germain, designed by the architect François d'Orbay, that Paris acquired its first theatre in which the auditorium was shaped in the form of an ellipse. Up till then the other theatres—the Hôtel de Bourgogne and the Palais Royal as well as those that were converted *jeux de paume*—had all been rectangular. We know from plans for their reconstruction in the 1640s which have survived that the interior of both the Hôtel de Bourgogne and the Théâtre du Marais was long and narrow—some 109 feet by 44 in the first case and approximately 120 feet by 39 in the second. Such a shape must have meant that many of the spectators found difficulty in seeing and hearing what was happening on the stage.

The accommodation provided for the audience was also somewhat different from what we are accustomed to today. The pit (*parterre*) offered mainly standing room though there were benches along the walls; this part of the theatre was an exclusively masculine preserve. Round three sides of the auditorium were arranged rows of boxes (*loges*); at first there were only two of these, but later a third row was added. Behind the *parterre* and below the boxes rose up a number of rows of seats known as the *amphithéâtre*; these were more expensive than a ticket to the *parterre* and indeed were at times frequented by quite illustrious personages.[1]

The most bizarre feature of a seventeenth-century Paris theatre in modern eyes was the presence of spectators on the stage itself. Though, in contrast to the London theatres of Shakespeare's day, there is no mention in any contemporary documents of their presence there in the opening decades of the century, they would appear to have become established there by the 1630s, perhaps at first only when a play was exceptionally successful, and then permanently—so much so that they were not removed from the stage of the Comédie Française until 1759.

In the 1650s Tallemant des Réaux wrote in his *Historiettes*:

[1] See below, pp.92–3. As there is some confusion about the exact location of the *amphithéâtre*, it might be as well to quote Furetière's dictionary (1690): 'se dit d'un lieu élevé vis-à-vis du théâtre, d'où l'on voit commodément la comédie; il est au-dessous des loges et plus haut que le parterre'.

Il y a à cette heure une incommodité épouvantable à la comédie; c'est que les deux côtés du théâtre sont tout pleins de jeunes gens assis sur des chaises de paille; cela vient de ce qu'ils ne veulent pas aller au parterre, quoiqu'il y ait souvent des soldats à la porte, et que les pages ni les laquais ne portent plus d'épées. Les loges sont fort chères, et il y faut songer de bonne heure: pour un écu, ou pour un demi-louis, on est sur le théâtre; mais cela gâte tout, et il ne faut quelquefois qu'un insolent pour tout troubler.[1]

If a play was not particularly successful, there might be very few spectators competing for space with the actors, but if the performance attracted a large audience, there could be a stage crowded with spectators, standing as well as seated.

Thus as the century progressed the arrangement of the auditorium gradually became more complicated. The register kept by Hubert at Molière's theatre in the Palais Royal for the theatrical year 1672/73 (a third row of boxes had only recently been added) lists sales of the following types of tickets:

> Théâtre
> Loges
> Amphithéâtre
> Loges hautes
> Loges du 3ᵉ rang
> Parterre.

At the opening performance given in 1680 by the newly constituted Comédie Française at the Théâtre Guénégaud there was a similar choice for the spectator:

> Théâtre
> Premières loges
> Amphithéâtre
> Secondes loges
> Troisièmes loges
> Parterre.[2]

The stage was raised well above the level of the *parterre* (just over 6 feet at both the Hôtel de Bourgogne and the Théâtre du Marais), presumably in an endeavour to keep the more unruly spectators at a safe distance from the actors, though this does not always seem to have prevented them from climbing up on to it in moments of drunken excitement. We know what was

---

[1] Vol. vii, p. 128. [2] S. Chevalley, *Album Théâtre classique*, p. 214.

the approximate size of the stage at these two theatres from the time of their reconstruction in the 1640s: in both it stretched across the whole width of the building (44 feet and 39 feet respectively). At the Hôtel de Bourgogne its depth was approximately 45 feet, and at the Théâtre du Marais roughly 42.

At the Hôtel de Bourgogne there was also towards the back a second stage raised up above the first (several of the leases specifically speak of 'théâtres' in the plural), and the contract for the reconstruction of the Théâtre du Marais in 1644 is quite explicit on the subject of this second stage: 'Au-dessus dudit théâtre il en faut faire un autre distant du premier de douze pieds de haut et de la même largeur du premier soutenu de huit piliers . . . Ledit second théâtre ne doit avoir que deux toises de long au milieu et aux côtés de trois toises.'[1] Quite how this second stage was used is a problem which historians of the theatre have not yet solved. As none of the theatres of the time were large, it is not easy to imagine how the stage could accommodate spectators as well as the actors and the necessary scenery.

Since neither gas nor electricity was yet available for lighting purposes, both the auditorium and, during performances, the stage had to be illuminated by candles. Snuffing all these candles so as to prevent them from making a most unpleasant smell was quite a large task which, Chappuzeau explains, was the responsibility of the scene-painters:

C'est aussi aux décorateurs de pourvoir de deux moucheurs pour les lumières, s'ils ne veulent pas eux-mêmes s'employer à cet office. Soit eux, soit d'autres, ils doivent s'en acquitter promptement, pour ne pas faire languir l'auditeur entre les actes; et avec propreté pour ne pas lui donner de mauvaise odeur. L'un mouche le devant du théâtre, et l'autre le fond, et surtout ils ont l'œil que le feu ne prenne aux toiles. Pour prévenir cet accident, on a soin de tenir toujours des muids pleins d'eau, et nombre de seaux, comme l'on en voit dans les places publiques des villes bien policées, sans attendre le mal pour courir à la rivière ou aux puits. Les restes des lumières font partie des petits profits des décorateurs.[2]

It has been suggested that what above all limited the separate acts of a seventeenth-century play to something like half an hour was the necessity for snuffing the candles in the theatre at

---

[1] Deierkauf-Holsboer, *Le Théâtre du Marais*, vol. i, pp. 194–5.
[2] *Le Théâtre français*, p. 149.

such intervals of time. More important, such a primitive form of illumination obviously ruled out the striking lighting effects which can be achieved in a modern theatre.

The actors also employed musicians to entertain the audience during the intervals between the acts, as Chappuzeau explains in some detail:

Les violons sont ordinairement au nombre de six et on les choisit les plus capables. Ci-devant on les plaçait ou derrière le théâtre ou sur les ailes ou dans un retranchement entre le théâtre et le parterre, comme en une forme de parquet. Depuis peu on les met dans une des loges du fond, d'où ils font plus de bruit que de tout autre lieu où on les pourrait placer. Il est bon qu'ils sachent par cœur les deux derniers vers de l'acte, pour reprendre promptement la symphonie sans attendre que l'on leur crie: 'Jouez!', ce qui arrive souvent.[1]

In the section headed 'Distributrices des douces liqueurs' Chappuzeau also tells us that a theatre in his day provided during the intervals the refreshments offered by the bar today; only what was offered and how it was offered were not quite what we are accustomed to:

Il me reste à dire un mot de la distributrice des liqueurs et des confitures, qui occupe deux places, l'une près des loges, et l'autre au parterre, où elle se tient, donnant la première à gouverner par commission. Ces places sont ornées de petits lustres, de quantité de beaux vases et de verres de cristal. On y tient l'été toutes sortes de liqueurs qui refraîchissent, des limonades, de l'aigre de cèdre,[2] des eaux de framboise, de groseille et de cerise, plusieurs confitures sèches, des citrons, des oranges de la Chine;[3] et l'hiver on y trouve des liqueurs qui réchauffent l'estomac, du rossolis de toutes les sortes, des vins d'Espagne et de La Scioutad, de Rivesaltes et de Saint-Laurent. J'ai vu le temps que l'on ne tenait dans ces mêmes lieux que de la bière et de la simple tisane, sans distinction de romaine et de citronnée; mais tout va en ce monde de bien en mieux, et de quelque côté que l'on se tourne, Paris ne fut jamais si beau ni si pompeux qu'il l'est aujourd'hui. Ces distributrices doivent être propres et civiles, et sont nécessaires à la comédie où chacun n'est pas d'humeur à demeurer trois heures sans se réjouir le goût par quelque douce liqueur.[4]

Interesting as this passage may be, nevertheless one would have preferred Chappuzeau to have given us more information about

---

[1] Ibid., pp. 146-7.
[2] 'On appelle aussi *cèdre* une espèce de citrons dont se fait une certaine boisson que l'on nomme *aigre de cèdre*' (*Dictionnaire de l'Académie française*, 1694).
[3] Sweet oranges (they did not come from China).
[4] *Le Théâtre français*, pp. 151-2.

the seventeenth-century spectator saw on the stage.

He has, for instance, not a word about the much debated question as to whether there was such a thing as a stage curtain in the theatres of his day, and if so, when it was introduced and how it was used. There is evidence that a stage curtain was in use quite early in the century for the performance of ballets at court, and the frontispiece of the play performed at the opening of Richelieu's theatre in the Palais Cardinal in 1641 shows a stage curtain. On the other hand the earliest mention of a stage curtain in a public theatre occurs in the contract for the work to be done at the Hôtel de Bourgogne when the interior of the building was remodelled in 1647 on the lines of the reconstruction of the Théâtre du Marais three years earlier. The agreement contains the words: 'Plus il faudra deux tirants au-devant du théâtre pour attacher la frise et l'élèvement du rideau distants l'un de l'autre de dix-huit pouces ou environ.'[1]

A stage curtain was then in use in the public theatres at any rate by the 1640s and possibly earlier. Even then the use made of it was very different from what we are accustomed to. Down to the end of the eighteenth century it does not appear to have been used to separate the acts or even scenes as it is nowadays, but simply to have been raised at the beginning of the performance and not lowered again until the end. In other words the stage and its setting lay revealed to the audience from one end of the play to the other. If the curtain had been lowered at the end of each act, it would not have been necessary for Chappuzeau to warn the musicians that they should memorize the last two lines of each act in order to avoid failing to strike up at the right moment.[2] In his *Pratique du Théâtre*, when dealing with the intervals between the acts, Abbé D'Aubignac points out that the playwright must avoid

une faute très grossière et néanmoins très commune aux nouveaux poètes, qui est de supposer dans l'intervalle d'un acte une chose qui ne peut vraisemblablement avoir été faite sans être vue; ce qui arrive quand on suppose qu'elle a été faite dans le lieu de la scène, car étant ouvert et exposé aux yeux des spectateurs, ils doivent vraisemblablement avoir vu tout ce qui s'y passe, ou bien il n'est pas vraisemblable que cette chose y soit arrivée puisqu'ils ne l'y ont pas vue.[3]

[1] Deierkauf-Holsboer, *Le Théâtre de l'Hôtel de Bourgogne*, vol. ii, p. 184.
[2] See above, p. 62.
[3] *La Pratique du théâtre*, ed. P. Martino (Algiers–Paris, 1927), p. 238.

The stage curtain was obviously a new invention and one which was not to be fully exploited until very much later.

There is no question but that in the course of the century a considerable change took place in the stage setting offered to the audiences of the period. We are extremely fortunate in having preserved for us details about stage settings at the Hôtel de Bourgogne and the Comédie Française at various periods between the 1630s and the 1680s.[1] For most of the plays of the period which are still well known today the setting, since they observe unity of place, was perfectly straightforward. The tragedies of Racine, for instance, when put on at the Hôtel de Bourgogne in 1678 required only one setting, described in the notes of the stage designer, Michel Laurent, in the following terms:

Andromaque. Théâtre est un palais à colonnes et, dans le fond, une mer avec des vaisseaux.
Britannicus. Théâtre est un palais à volonté.
Bérénice. Le théâtre est un petit cabinet royal.
Bajazet. Le théâtre est un salon à la turque.
Mithridate. Le théâtre est un palais à volonté.
Iphigénie. Théâtre est des tentes et, dans le fond, une mer et des vaisseaux.
Phèdre. Théâtre est un palais voûté.[2]

The comedies of Molière, when performed in this theatre at this same date, generally presented no difficulty as they too observed unity of place. The setting for both *Le Misanthrope* and *Tartuffe* is described very simply as 'Théâtre est une chambre', while all that was needed for *L'Avare* was 'une salle et, sur le derrière, un jardin'. The setting for *L'École des femmes* was an outdoor one: 'Théâtre est deux maisons sur le devant et le reste est une place de ville.'[3]

As late as this period in the century strict unity of place was not, however, always observed, even in tragedy. For instance, Thomas Corneille's *Le Comte d'Essex*, first performed in this very year 1678, required a change of scene: 'Théâtre est un palais et une prison qui paraît au quatrième acte.'[4]

---

[1] *Le Mémoire de Mahelot, Laurent et d'autres décorateurs de l'Hôtel de Bourgogne et de la Comédie Française au XVIIᵉ siècle,* ed. H. C. Lancaster (Paris, 1920).
[2] Ibid., pp. 112-14.   [3] Ibid., pp. 118-19.
[4] Ibid., pp. 114-15.

A contract signed in 1664 for the scenery of Molière's *Dom Juan* which has been miraculously preserved gives a detailed description of the variety of settings required for this particular play:

Devis des ouvrages de peinture qu'il convient faire pour Messieurs les comédiens de Monseigneur le duc d'Orléans, frère unique du Roi.

Premièrement un palais consistant en cinq châssis[1] de chaque côté et une façade contre la poutre, au travers duquel l'on verra deux châssis de jardin et le fond, dont le premier châssis aura dix-huit pieds de haut et tous les autres en diminuant en perspective.

Plus un hameau de verdure consistant en cinq châssis de chaque côté, le premier de dix-huit pieds et tous les autres en diminuant de perspective, et une grotte pour cacher la poutre au travers de laquelle on verra deux châssis de mer et le fond.

Plus une forêt consistant en trois châssis de chaque côté dont le premier sera de dix-huit pieds et les autres en diminuant, et un châssis, fermant sur lequel sera peint une manière de temple entouré de verdure.

Plus le dedans d'un temple consistant en cinq châssis de chaque côté dont le premier sera dix-huit pieds de haut et les autres en diminuant et un châssis fermant, contre la poutre, représentant le fond du temple.

Plus une chambre consistant en trois châssis de chaque côté dont le premier sera de dix-huit pieds de haut et les autres en diminuant et un châssis fermant représentant le fond de la chambre.

Plus une ville consistant en cinq châssis de chaque côté, dont le premier sera de dix-huit pieds et les autres en diminuant, un châssis contre la poutre où sera peinte une porte de ville et deux petits châssis de ville aussi et le fond.

Plus quatre bandes de ciel traversant le théâtre.

Plus quatre frises, manière de voûte, traversant aussi le théâtre.

Plus une cintre de deux pilastres et une frise par le devant du théâtre.

Plus deux petits balcons qu'il faudra orner.

Plus un petit plafond qu'il faudra rafraîchir.

Sera fourni aux entrepreneurs les châssis tendus de toiles et cartons prêts à travailler.[2]

In comparison the description of the scenery for this play as put on at the Comédie Française in the 1680s, not in Molière's original prose, but in the verse of Thomas Corneille, is rather laconic, but it does, of course reflect the frequent changes of scene:

1er acte, il faut un palais.

2e acte, une chambre, une mer.

3e un bois, un tombeau.

4e une chambre.

5e le tombeau paraît, il faut une trappe.[3]

---

[1] In theatrical parlance 'flats', i.e. sections of scenery mounted on frames.

[2] M. Jurgens and M. Maxfield-Miller, *Cent ans de recherches sur Molière* (Paris, 1963), pp. 399–400.   [3] *Le Mémoire de Mahelot*, p. 125.

Such changes of scene had by this period in the century become exceptional, but they were normal practice when Pierre
Corneille and the young playwrights of his generation began
writing for the stage around 1630. We are remarkably well informed about the stage settings of this period thanks to the
survival of the *Mémoire de Mahelot*. Not only did Laurent
Mahelot provide much more detailed notes than his successors
about the settings of the plays in the repertoire of the Hôtel de
Bourgogne in 1634; he also left behind for the benefit of posterity no fewer than forty-seven sketches of these settings.

Very occasionally, it is true, these show that only one picture
was presented to the audience from beginning to end just as
with later classical plays; but in general the stage setting represented, not in succession as in the examples quoted above, but
simultaneously a number of quite different places. In other
words, in the 1630s the Hôtel de Bourgogne and presumably
also the Théâtre du Marais continued to make use of the so-called
multiple setting (*décor simultané*) inherited from the medieval
stage where it had been used for more spacious outdoor performances. Another difference from medieval usage was that
under Italian influence use was made of perspective to blend the
setting into a coherent whole. One has to imagine quite a number of different places being represented simultaneously on the
stage with the actors moving from one section to another as the
scene changed, but probably also performing on the front of
the stage.

To take one or two examples, we find Mahelot describing the
following setting for Rotrou's comedy, *La Bague de l'oubli*:

Il faut un palais au milieu du théâtre qui soit en rotonde avec des balustres.
Il faut une chambre garnie d'une table avec un tapis dessus, un tableau
dans la chambre, un bassin à laver avec une aiguière ou vase, une serviette.
Pour l'autre côté du théâtre il faut qu'il ait une grotte, fontaine, jardin,
fleurs. A côté du jardin et du palais, il faut un échafaud tendu de noir
qui soit caché; il s'ouvre au cinquième acte, à la première scène.[1]

The scaffold, it will be noted, was to be kept hidden until the
beginning of the fifth act; this was done by means of a curtain
covering the part of the setting which it was necessary to hide

[1] *Le Mémoire de Mahelot*, p. 69.

from the spectator until the action required it. Changes of scene were particularly numerous in the very popular genre of tragi-comedy, as for instance in Pierre Du Ryer's *Clitophon* which, it will be seen, also makes use of a curtain to hide part of the setting:

Au milieu du théâtre un temple fort superbe, qui sert au cinquième acte, est le plus beau du théâtre, enrichi de lierre, d'or clinquant, balustres, termes ou colonnes, un tableau de Diane au milieu de l'autel, deux chand-eliers garnis de chandelles. A un côté du théâtre il faut une prison en tour ronde; que la grille soit fort grande et basse pour voir trois prisonniers. A côté de la prison il faut un beau jardin spacieux orné de balustres, de fleurs et de palissades. De l'autre côté du théâtre il faut une montagne élevée; sur ladite montagne un tombeau, un pilier, un carcan, et un autel bocager de verdure et rocher où l'on puisse monter sur ledit rocher devant le peuple. A côté du rocher un antre, une mer, un demi-vaisseau. Sous le rocher faire paraître une prison pour deux personnes, qui soit cachée.[1]

Another example of the numerous changes of scene represented in one setting is provided by Mahelot's notes for D'Auvray's tragicomedy, *Dorinde*:

Au milieu du théâtre il faut la forteresse de Marcilly, haute de cinq pieds, où se livre l'assaut . . . Au-dessous de la forteresse forme de casemate dans la contre-escarpe; à ladite casemate il faut une grille qui s'ouvre et ferme. A un des côtés du théâtre il faut une tente de guerre, un passage, une tour, une corde nouée pour descendre de la tour, un pont-levis qui se lâche quand il est nécessaire. De l'autre côté. un bois et une grotte, case de bergère, une mer.[2]

There is no question but that these frequent changes of scene which, of course, implied a complete rejection of unity of place, were extremely popular in the early part of the century. How-ever, the continued existence of the multiple setting is of little interest to the average student of seventeenth-century drama who, quite justifiably, is content to leave almost all plays before *Le Cid* to be read by specialists in theatre history.

Le Cid, however, first performed at the Théâtre du Marais in 1637, is interesting from this point of view as from many others. It is notorious that this play—first given out not as a tragedy, but as a tragicomedy—is a kind of half-way house between the type of drama fashionable around 1630 and the new type of

[1] Ibid., pp. 85–6. [2] Ibid., pp. 81–2.

drama based on the famous Classical rules. Although Corneille made a tremendous effort to concentrate the action of the play which he derived from his Spanish model, its unity is impaired by the role of the Infanta. Unity of time is strictly observed, but the result is that an extraordinary amount of action is crowded into this short space of time. After relating the numerous incidents in the play—the quarrel between the two fathers, the duel between Rodrique and the Count, Rodrique's victory over the Moors, and his duel with Don Sanche—Scudéry concludes ironically: 'Je vous laisse à juger si ne voilà pas un jour bien employé et si l'on n'aurait pas grand tort d'accuser tous ces personnages de paresse.'[1]

The setting of *Le Cid* in Seville in which town Corneille concentrated all the action of his play in order to make some attempt to observe unity of place obviously required a multiple setting very different from the conventional antechamber in a palace of his later tragedies or of those of Racine. To grasp how the stage appeared to a spectator at the Théâtre du Marais in 1637 we have to visualize the king's apartment, that of the Infanta, the street, and Chimène's house all being represented simultaneously on the stage and the actors performing in or near the appropriate setting.

Even contemporaries found it difficult to locate the action of *Le Cid* with any precision. Scudéry, as might be expected of a very hostile critic, denounced the play from this point of view: 'Le théâtre en est si mal entendu qu'un même lieu représentant l'appartement du Roi, celui de l'Infante, la maison de Chimène et la rue, presque sans changer de face, le spectateur ne sait le plus souvent où en sont les acteurs'.[2] Corneille himself when he wrote *Le Cid* does not seem to have had a very clear notion of which part of the setting was involved for certain scenes in the play. Writing his *Examen* of *Le Cid* some twenty years later, he has to confess that at times the exact place of the action is decidedly obscure:

Tout s'y passe donc dans Séville, et garde ainsi quelque espèce d'unité de lieu en général; mais le lieu particulier change de scène en scène, et tantôt c'est le palais du Roi, tantôt l'appartement de l'Infante, tantôt la maison

[1] *La Querelle du 'Cid'*, pp. 77–8.   [2] Ibid., p. 95.

de Chimène, et tantôt une rue ou place publique. On le détermine aisément pour les scènes détachées; mais pour celles qui ont leur liaison ensemble, comme les quatre dernières du premier acte, il est malaisé d'en choisir un qui convienne à toutes.

In the four scenes in question we see the two fathers together in sc.3, then in sc.4 Don Diègue alone; in sc.5 he is joined by his son, and in sc.6 Rodrique is left alone on the stage; but as Corneille himself admits, it is difficult to determine exactly where these four scenes take place:

Le Comte et Don Diègue se querellent au sortir du palais; cela se peut passer dans une rue; mais après le soufflet reçu, Don Diègue ne peut pas demeurer en cette rue à faire ses plaintes, attendant que son fils survienne, qu'il ne soit tout aussitôt environné de peuple, et ne reçoive l'offre de quelques amis. Il serait plus à propos qu'il se plaignît dans sa maison.

The solution which he offers—it has certain analogies with the technique of the cinema—is an ingenious one:

Ainsi, par une fiction de théâtre, on peut s'imaginer que Don Diègue et le Comte, sortant du palais du Roi, avancent toujours en se querellant, et sont arrivés devant la maison de ce premier lorsqu'il reçoit le soufflet qui l'oblige à y entrer pour y chercher du secours.

Act V of *Le Cid* also produces its complications. Scene 1 takes place in Chimène's house, sc.s 2 and 3 in the Infanta'a apartment. Scene 4 between Chimène and Elvire presumably takes place in Chimène's house, like sc. 5 in which she receives a visit from Don Sanche. Yet immediately afterwards in sc.6 we find her in the royal palace in the presence of the king and his court where the final scene of the play takes place. How she gets from one setting to another between line 1722 in which she is addressing Don Sanche in her own house and line 1723 where she is addressing the king in the royal palace is a mystery. As Corneille does not tell us, we have no idea of what happened on the stage of the Théâtre du Marais in 1637 at this point in the play, but it is clear that, in reading *Le Cid* today, we must try to imagine the action played against a multiple setting, so different from the 'palais à volonté' of later Classical tragedies.

The costumes which the actors and actesses wore on the stage in seventeenth-century Paris no doubt varied both in the course of the century according to the prosperity or otherwise of the theatre and according to the type of play in which they happened to be performing.

The evidence for the opening decades of the century in which the theatre was far from prosperous is, as usual, extremely scrappy and difficult to interpret. Yet the documents miraculously assembled by Mme Deierkauf-Holsboer concerning the actor Valleran Le Conte who made various appearances in Paris between 1598 and 1612 would seem to indicate that even he had a stock of costumes of some value; in agreements which he signed he was to supply them for the whole company. From the 1630s onwards we have inventories made on the marriage or death of a number of actors, including Molière, and there is no doubt that they could possess extremely expensive costumes. Those of Molière, though numerous, were not particularly valuable; oddly enough, the inventory of his possessions does not include any of the costumes he wore when performing in trage-dies, though he had often acted in them. In contrast, as early as 1637 we find in the inventory made after the death of Charles Lenoir, the leading actor of the Théâtre du Marais, some much more expensive costumes, the valuation rising for one of them to as much as the considerable sum of 300 livres. His actress wife too had some valuable items, including 'une robe de satin noir toute couverte de broderie d'or et d'argent en relief', put down as being worth 450 livres.[1] Molière's widow also had a fair number of stage costumes, the most expensive being those she wore in *Psyché* which were valued at 250 livres. However, all these expensive costumes were far outshone by those of Molière's actor, La Grange; when on his marriage in 1672 an inventory of his possessions was drawn up, it included some extraordinarily rich costumes, two of them being put down at no less than 900 livres.[2]

However, it is by no means easy for a twentieth-century reader of these inventories to visualize exactly what the costumes, male and female, looked like on the stage. On paper one should derive a great deal of assistance from the frontispieces of the plays published in this period as they generally offered an engraving of some scene in the play; but whether the artist was attempting an exact reproduction of the scene and the costumes worn by

[1] Deierkauf-Holsboer, *Le Théâtre du Marais*, vol. i, pp. 163-8.
[2] Jurgens and Maxfield-Miller, *Cent ans de recherches sur Molière*, pp. 566-71, 711-12.

the actors or simply drawing on his imagination we have no means of telling.

What sort of costumes were worn in comedy is, of course, fairly clear. Nowadays the comedies of Molière are occasionally performed in modern dress, but more often in costumes which are, at any rate approximately, a reconstruction of the costumes of a bygone age. Obviously in the seventeenth century his comedies and those of the numerous other playwrights of the age, since they dealt with contemporary subjects, were performed in the costumes of the time. As the characters, both male and female, were drawn from a great variety of social classes, the costumes worn varied considerably. In the part of a nobleman like Alceste Molière wore an appropriately expensive outfit— 'haut-de-chausses et justaucorps de brocart rayé or et soie gris, doublé de tabis, garni de ruban vert, la veste de brocart d'or, les bas de soie et jarretières'. In the part of a wealthy bourgeois like Orgon in *Tartuffe* he wore a more sober outfit—'pourpoint, chausses et manteau de vénitienne noire, le manteau doublé de tabis et garni de dentelle d'Angleterre, les jarretières et ronds de souliers et souliers pareillement garnis', while in the part of Harpagon he wore clothes appropriate to an old miser—'un manteau, chausses et pourpoint de satin noir, garni de dentelle ronde de soie noire, chapeau, perruque, souliers'. There is a well-known contemporary engraving of Molière in the part of Sganarelle, a character who keeps on appearing in six different comedies down to *Le Médecin malgré lui*; however, the inventory of his possessions shows that he had a whole series of costumes for this part in the different plays, as was only natural since Sganarelle's social position varied from that of a prosperous bourgeois to a peasant. In the part of Mascarille in his early plays, including *Les Précieuses ridicules*, Molière wore a mask in the tradition of earlier farce actors (the name means 'little mask'), but he no longer wore one in the part of Sganarelle. Actresses too wore contemporary costumes corresponding to the social position of the characters whom they were portraying.

What sort of costumes were worn in tragedy is much less clear. It is only very rarely that we have precise documentary evidence to help us to form a clear picture of what the actors and actresses wore; and even then we are left in doubt as to its precise meaning.

For Racine's tragedy, *Bajazet,* the action of which takes place not in ancient Greece or Rome, but in seventeenth-century Turkey, the Hôtel de Bourgogne provided 'un salon à la turque', and Corneille who was present at one of the early performances of Racine's play is alleged to have said that all the characters 'ont, *sous un habit turc*, le sentiment qu'on a au milieu de la France'.[1] In 1747, Racine's son, Louis, stated that at the Comédie Française the play was performed with 'des robes longues et des turbans',[2] and in this the actors may well have been following a tradition which went back to the play's first run in 1672. Even so, the modern reader is left wondering exactly what they understood by either 'un salon à la turque' or 'un habit turc'.

The great majority of seventeenth-century tragedies were, of course, set in ancient Greece or Rome, but here again to try to visualize the sort of costumes worn by actors and actresses is a difficult task. The whole problem is one which has to be set in historical perspective. In the second half of the eighteenth century attempts were made at the Comédie Française, partly under the influence of Voltaire, to move towards greater historical accuracy in both the costumes and settings of the plays performed there. The great name associated with this change is that of Talma who began his career at the Comédie Française shortly before the Revolution. Writing in the 1760s in his commentary on Corneille, Voltaire has some amusing remarks to offer on the subject of the lack of historical realism in the costumes traditionally worn in performances of *Polyeucte* at the Comédie Française. The action of the play takes place in Armenia in the reign of the Roman emperor, Decius, in the third century A.D. Yet when (Act IV, sc. 3) Polyeucte prays to God for the conversion of his wife, Pauline, to Christianity, Voltaire comments: 'Je me souviens qu'autrefois l'acteur qui jouait Polyeucte, avec des gants blancs et un grand chapeau, ôtait ses gants et son chapeau pour faire sa prière à Dieu.' Again the last scene of the play in which the Roman, Sévère, joins Félix, the Roman senator and governor of Armenia, provokes another amusing reminiscence of earlier days at the Comédie Française (Voltaire was born in 1694 and his first tragedy was performed in 1718): 'Autrefois, quand les

---

[1] J.R. de Segrais, *Œuvres* (Paris, 1755, 2 vols.), vol. ii, p. 43.
[2] *Œuvres* (Paris, 1743-7, 4 vols.), vol. ii, p. 283.

acteurs représentaient les Romains avec le chapeau et une cravate, Sévère arrivait le chapeau sur la tête, Félix l'écoutait chapeau bas, ce qui faisait un effet ridicule.'[1] Another revealing eighteenth-century account of the way ancient Rome was portrayed at the Comédie Française is provided by Louis-Sébastien Mercier. The anecdote concerns the scene in Corneille's *Horace* in which hurling imprecations at Rome after the death of her Alban fiancé, Curiace, Camille is chased off the stage by her brother, Horace, and murdered in the wings:

La Duclos[2] jouait dans les *Horaces*. A la fin de ses imprécations, elle sort furieuse, comme l'on sait; l'actrice s'embarrassa dans la queue très longue de sa robe et tomba. On vit soudain l'acteur qui faisait Horace ôter poliment son chapeau d'une main, la relever de l'autre, la reconduire dans la coulisse, et là, remettant fièrement son chapeau, tirer son épée et la tuer, conformément à son rôle.

To this he adds the significant explanatory footnote; 'Les acteurs tragiques portaient, dans toutes les tragédies, un chapeau surmonté de plumes; et c'est ainsi qu'on a joué en France pendant près de cent ans Corneille et Racine.'[3] It seems clear that until well into the eighteenth century the average theatregoer was quite content to see actors and actresses dressed in a vaguely Graeco-Roman costume even if the men wore with it wigs and plumed hats. Writing in 1747 Louis Racine could declare: 'Un savant peut trouver à redire qu'Achille, sur le théâtre, soit habillé comme Auguste et Mithridate; et il sait que ces trois princes étaient habillés différemment; mais le peuple, qui l'ignore, n'est pas même choqué de leur voir à tous trois des perruques et des chapeaux.'[4]

The actors and actresses who appeared in the tragedies performed in the theatres of seventeenth-century Paris certainly did not wear simply what could be called 'modern dress'. The inventories of their possessions variously describe the costumes they wore in plays set in ancient Greece or Rome as 'à l'antique' or, using the same term as Chappuzeau,[5] 'à la romaine'. These were obviously somewhat conventional adaptations of what was

---

[1] *Complete Works,* vol. liv, pp. 330, 344.
[2] An actress at the Comédie Française from 1693 to 1733.
[3] *Tableau de Paris* (Amsterdam, 1783–9, 12 vols.), vol. iii, p. 9.
[4] *Œuvres,* vol. ii, p. 283.   [5] See above, p. 27.

known of the clothes worn by Greek and Roman men and women. The main point seems to have been that the costumes should appear rich and impressive on the stage. In 1637 the actor Lenoir possessed 'une casaque à l'antique' which was described as being 'de satin jaune tout couvert de broderies d'argent doublé de panne jaune avec les bottines, éperon et garniture de même'.[1] The most expensive costumes of Molière's widow, Armande, were those she wore in the *tragédie-ballet, Psyché*, which was given its first performance in the Tuileries palace before Louis XIV:

Les habits pour la représentation de *Psyché*, consistant en une jupe de toile d'or garnie de trois dentelles d'argent avec un corps en broderie et garni d'un tonnelet et manches d'or et d'argent fin, une autre jupe de toile d'argent dont le devant garni de plusieurs dentelles d'argent fin avec une mante de crêpe garnie de pareille dentelle et une autre jupe de moire verte et argent, garnie de dentelle fausse avec le corps en broderie, le tonnelet et les manches garnis d'or et d'argent fin, une autre jupe de taffetas d'Angleterre bleu, garni de quatre dentelles d'argent fin.[2]

The actor, La Grange, in the same company owned no fewer than three different 'habits à l'antique', the most splendid of which is described as being 'de broderie d'argent fin, fort relevé, consistant en corps, lambrequins, tonnelette, brodequins, manches, coiffures et garnitures, couleur de cerise'.[3] Another of Molière's actors (he abandoned the company in 1673 and went over to the Hôtel de Bourgogne) possessed what is described as 'un habit à la romaine, consistant en un corps tonnelette de lambrequin, un petit tonnelet à dessus noir, le tout d'argent fin, un grand bas de soie de gris de perle, une paire de gants garni d'une dentelle d'argent fine, pourpoint blanc garni d'une dentelle d'argent fine et des tours de bras de point de Paris, brodé d'or, festons et dentelles d'argent fine, le tout garni, d'un petit ruban noir et blanc et un bouquet de plume bleue'.[4] Again, we know that the great tragic actress, La Champmeslé, possessed no fewer than seven 'habits à la romaine'. One of these (it was particularly rich, being valued at the enormous sum of 1,100 livres) consisted of 'un corps et une veste à fond bleu et fleurs d'or, une jupe de

---

[1] Deierkauf-Holsboer, *Le Théâtre du Marais*, vol. i, p. 165.
[2] Jurgens and Maxfield-Miller, *Cent ans de recherches sur Molière*, p. 570.
[3] Ibid., p. 711.
[4] Ibid., p. 715.

raz d'argent, garnie d'un grand falbala de point d'Espagne d'or', and another was described as 'tout complet de velours vert, brodé d'or et argent, avec une grande frange d'or à double rang, le tout fin, prisé avec le sabre à poignée d'argent et le fourreau aussi à plaque d'argent, bout et chaîne, le tout d'orfèvrerie: 500 livres'.[1]

Even if it is impossible to visualize from these descriptions exactly what the costumes worn in tragedy by the actors and actresses of the time looked like under the candelebra lighting up the stage, it is clear that, while rightly or wrongly, no attempt was made at exact reproduction of the dress of male and female characters in tragedies set in ancient Greece or Rome, the costumes were not exactly the equivalent of modern dress, even if, as we have seen, the actors wore or carried hats with large plumes. The costumes worn were purely conventional ones, distinguished above all for their richness and for the impression of splendour and elegance which they would make on the spectator.

Such, in broad outline, is the picture which we can today form of what it was like to be inside a seventeenth-century Paris theatre. Although there are unfortunately many gaps in our knowledge, we can still by an effort of imagination re-create for ourselves, as we read the plays of writers like Corneille, Molière, and Racine, the sort of theatres in which they were first performed and also see how certain features of them were influenced by the material conditions under which the actors and behind them the playwrights of the age had to work. Another important influence was exercised on them by the audiences to which both sought to appeal.

[1] Quoted in J. Heuzey, 'Du costume et de la décoration tragique au XVIIᵉ siècle', *Revue d'histoire du théâtre*, 1960, p. 30.

IV Audiences

Even if the seventeenth-century playwright probably gave no thought to the spectators in the despised provinces, he had to bear in mind that he was writing for two rather different, if overlapping audiences—that of the court and that of the public theatres of Paris. From one end of the century to the other, the king and court took an interest in drama either by having plays performed in the royal palaces in Paris or Versailles or even occasionally in the provinces or else by attending the public theatres.

It is true that the interest shown by the king and court in drama was greater in some periods of the century than in others, it is also better documented in certain reigns. We know very little about the interest shown by Henry IV in the theatre at a period when, it must be remembered, it was not yet the fashionable entertainment it was later to become. Yet we do know that he and his Italian queen, Marie de Médicis, went to great trouble to persuade companies from Italy to come to Paris and entertain them and their court. Moreover, in those days when French companies from the provinces could not long hold out at the Hôtel de Bourgogne, we find at least one reference to a visit paid to that theatre by Henry and his court. In January 1607 a contemporary noted in his Journal: 'Le vendredi 26e de ce mois fut jouée, à l'Hôtel de Bourgogne, à Paris, une plaisante farce, à laquelle assistèrent le roi, la reine, et la plupart des princes, seigneurs et dames de la cour.' [1] In 1609 and again in 1611, first as dauphin and then as king, the young Louis XIII was taken on several occasions to see plays at the Hôtel de Bourgogne.

If we know little of Louis XIII's visits to this theatre after his early youth, it is an interesting fact that Louis XIV did not disdain to frequent the public theatres of the capital, either

[1] P. de L'Estoile, *Mémoires-journaux*, ed. G. Brunet *et al.* (Paris, 1875–96, 12 vols.), vol. viii, p. 271.

before he took over the reins of power in 1661 or for some time afterwards. In 1656, for instance, when he was eighteen, he went to the Théâtre du Marais for a performance of Thomas Corneille's highly successful tragedy, *Timocrate*. Two years later Louis and his court went to the rival theatre of the Hôtel de Bourgogne for a performance of a lost tragedy and shortly afterwards saw a performance given by the Italian actors. At the beginning of 1659 they went to see Pierre Corneille's latest tragedy, *Œdipe*, again at the Hôtel de Bourgogne. Molière's theatre was not left out of these visits; in 1663, for instance, La Grange recorded the king's presence at a performance of *L'École des femmes* and *La Critique*: 'Le Roi nous honora de sa présence en public'; and six months later, in January 1664, we find the following entry: 'Joué dans notre salle au Palais Royal pour le Roi la *Bradamante ridicule*'.[1] In 1666 Louis attended a performance of Boyer's *pièce à machines, Jupiter et Sémélé,* at the Marais theatre which specialized in this type of production.

However, it was much more usual for plays to be performed in the royal palaces. Although our information about such performances in the first half of the century is decidedly scrappy, we catch occasional glimpses of both French and Italian actors performing at court during the reign of Henry IV. Such court performances continued during the reign of Louis XIII. We know of one particular period of intensive dramatic activity at court during his minority; in the space of fifteen months, between November 1612 and Febrary 1614, over 130 performances were given at court by professional actors, both French and Italian. Our information about theatrical performances at court during the rest of Louis XIII's reign and the regency which followed his death in 1643 is decidedly meagre, but there is no doubt that they took place fairly frequently.

It was, however, during the period between Louis XIV's assumption of power in 1661 and his estrangement from the theatre in his years of piety that the drama saw its most brilliant period at the French court in the seventeenth-century. After the death of his queen in 1683 and his attachment to Mme de Maintenon Louis gradually began to lose interest in the drama; in November 1691 the Marquis de Dangeau noted in his journal:

[1] pp. 58, 63.

'Le soir il y eut comédie; le roi n'y va plus du tout.'[1] Theatrical performances still continued at court in the latter part of the reign; even if they no longer took place with all the splendour of of the sumptuous fêtes of the 1660s and 1670s, they had become a regular part of the routine of life at court and were to remain so right down to the Revolution. At the high point of the reign most of the performances took place in Paris or later at Versailles when the court was permanently established there; in addition, they were sometimes given at Fontainebleau or other royal palaces in the provinces.

Not only did the king and court see performed new plays or older ones which had first been put on in the public theatres; quite a number of the plays of the time were given their first performance at court. Racine's first great success in tragedy, *Andromaque,* received its first performance not at the Hôtel de Bourgogne, but at the Louvre. The *Gazette de France* carried the following item on 19 November 1667: 'Leurs Majestés eurent le divertissement d'une fort belle tragédie, par la Troupe Royale, en l'appartement de la Reine, où étaient quantité de seigneurs et de dames de la cour.' Seven years later the *Gazette* announced another court première for a Racine play, *Iphigénie* (even managing to give the author's name on this occasion):

De Versailles, le 24 août 1674,
. . . Le soir, Leurs Majestés, avec lesquelles étaient Monseigneur le Dauphin, Monsieur, et un grand nombre de seigneurs et de dames, prirent ici, dans l'Orangerie, le divertissement d'une pièce nouvelle de théâtre intitulée *Iphigénie,* composée par le sieur Racine, laquelle fut admirablement bien représentée par la Troupe Royale et très applaudie de toute la Cour. Ensuite elles eurent aussi le divertissement d'un grand feu d'artifice sur le Canal.

When Molière and his company—known after their patron, Louis XIV's brother, as 'la Troupe de Monsieur'—made their return to Paris in 1658, the first performance which they gave in the capital was at the Louvre, as La Grange records in his register: 'La Troupe de Monsieur, frère unique du Roi, commença au Louvre devant sa Majesté le 24e octobre 1658 par *Nicomède* et *Le Docteur amoureux.*'[2]

Indeed in the fifteen years which followed down to his death

---

[1] *Journal,* ed. E. Soulié *et al.* (Paris, 1854–60, 19 vols.), vol. iii, p. 431.   [2] p. 1.

Molière became very much a court entertainer. If most of the plays—*Le Misanthrope* is a notable exception—which he put on first in the Petit Bourbon and Palais Royal theatres were given subsequently at court during his lifetime, quite a number received their first performance before the king, mostly as part of a more or less elaborate court entertainment.

The long and complicated history of the most successful of all his comedies, *Tartuffe*, began in 1664 when his company took part in the fêtes held at Versailles under the title of *Les Plaisirs de l'Ile enchantée*. His company's contribution consisted of performances of a new 'comédie galante mêlée de musique et d'entrées de ballet', *La Princesse d'Élide*, specially written for the occasion; a comedy, *Les Fâcheux*, first performed three years earlier at Vaux-le-Vicomte at a fête offered by Foucquet to Louis XIV; then, according to La Grange's register, 'trois actes du *Tartuffe* qui étaient les trois premiers'; and finally a *comédie-ballet*, *Le Mariage forcé*, in which the king had danced when it was performed in the Louvre a few months earlier.[1] Some of these court performances were given in royal palaces at quite a distance from Paris. Thus in 1670 the well-known *comédie-ballet, Le Bourgeois Gentilhomme*, received its first performance at Chambord, one of the royal palaces in the Loire valley, as La Grange records: 'La troupe est partie pour Chambord par ordre du Roi. On y a joué entre plusieurs comédies *Le Bourgeois gentilhomme*, pièce nouvelle de M. de Molière.'[2] The première took place on 14 October, and it was not until 23 November that the first public performance of this new play was given at the Palais Royal theatre.

Thanks to La Grange's register we are fairly well informed about the performances given at court by Molière's company and from this and other contemporary sources we know what they performed there, whether completely new plays or others which had had their first performance in Paris. From 1680 onwards we know from the registers of the Comédie Française exactly what court performances the new company gave. Unfortunately for the period before 1680 we have only rather scrappy information about the court performances given by companies like the Hôtel de Bourgogne. We must not, however, imagine

---

[1] p.67.   [2] p.118.

that Molière's company had anything like a monopoly of court performances between 1658 and 1673. We have seen, for instance, that *Andromaque* and *Iphigénie* were given their première at court by the rival company of the Hôtel de Bourgogne.

While it would no doubt be a mistake to imagine that all the spectators at these court performances were required to furnish written proof of their noble birth before being allowed in to enjoy the spectacle, it is pretty clear that such court audiences must have been markedly more aristocratic than those in the public theatres. Indeed for the opening decades of the century—a period of scarcely relieved darkness so far as the history of the theatre is concerned—it has often been argued that the spectators who frequented the Hôtel de Bourgogne and various improvised theatres were the very opposite of aristocratic. The striking thing about the plays of the opening part of the century—be they comedies, tragedies, tragicomedies, or pastoral plays—is their aesthetic and moral crudity. It is perhaps too easy to conclude that theatre audiences must therefore have been decidely plebeian, lacking the refining influence of the upper classes of society and especially that of respectable women. Tempting as this conclusion may be, it is not altogether borne out by the facts. The theatre was undoubtedly a much less fashionable entertainment than it was to become by about 1630; the plays produced were of little literary worth and were often extremely crude, even obscene, in their subject-matter and language. Yet though the theatre was a much cheaper form of entertainment than it was to become later in the century, there are fragments of evidence which indicate that audiences were much more mixed than is often suggested.

There is, for instance, some evidence that no only some young bloods of the aristocracy, but even some solid bourgeois attended the theatre in these decades. What is more, the documents on which historians of the theatre rely in order to exclude respectable women from audiences of the time are no more conclusive than those produced by scholars who attempt to do the same for the London theatres of Shakespeare's day. Thus the apparently categorical statement of Abbé d'Aubignac, writing in the 1660s, that 'il y a cinquante ans qu'une honnête femme n'osait aller au théâtre' is considerably modified by the rest of the sentence: 'ou bien il fallait qu'elle fût voilée et tout à fait invisible, et ce plaisir était comme réservé aux débauchées qui se donnaient la liberté de regarder à visage découvert.'[1] In other words d'Aubignac does admit that some 'honnêtes femmes' did go to the theatre in the opening decades of the century, even if they went veiled. Charles Sorel, writing a few years later, is even further from denying that respectable women were present in the theatre at that period in the century. 'Autrefois', he declares, 'toutes les femmes se retiraient quand on allait jouer la farce.'[2] Even if information about the composition of theatre audiences at the beginning of this period is extremely hard to come by, it would certainly seem rash to conclude that neither men of the upper classes of society nor respectable women frequented the theatre in these years.

We have seen that the attitude of the court of Henry IV and the young Louis XIII to drama was not as negative as has often been imagined. Meagre as our information undoubtedly is, it suffices to prove that in these years the court did not regard theatrical performances as entirely beneath contempt, as an entertainment suited only for the plebs, for a horde of ruffians, and dissolute women. Whether the king along with other members of the royal family and his courtiers, male and female, attended theatrical performances given in the various royal palaces or (this seems to have happened much less frequently) at that alleged place of perdition, the Hôtel de Bourgogne, there is no doubt that they saw exactly the same plays—French or Italian—as were presented to the ordinary spectators in the public theatre. Clearly we do not possess, for the opening decades of the seventeenth century, one set of crude plays written for the plebeian audiences of the Hôtel de Bourgogne and another set of refined plays written to please the more sophisticated taste of the court.

It is characteristic that the only two anecdotes in Tallement's *Historiettes* relating to Henry IV's interest in drama concern encounters with actors who were particularly distinguished for their roles in farce—Arlequin and Gros-Guillaume.[3] His Italian queen, Marie de Médicis, naturally took a keen interest in actors

---

[1] *Dissertation sur la condamnation des théâtres* (Paris, 1666), pp. 243-4.
[2] *De la connaissance des bons livres* (Amsterdam, 1672), p. 166.
[3] Vol. i, pp. 16, 17.

from her own country, but she seems also to have enjoyed performances by French actors, particularly in farce. After the
murder of her favourite, Concini, she endeavoured to while away
the time in her exile at Blois with visits from two well-known
farce actors. The accounts of her household show that in May
1618 the sum of 90 livres was paid to 'Robert Guérin, dit La
Fleur', better known as Gros-Guillaume, and in December of the
same year she gave 600 livres to 'Phillipe Mondor, médecin' and
to 'ceux qui l'ont assisté pour jouer les comédies qu'ils ont repré-
sentées diverses fois devant nous pour notre plaisir et service'.
Philippe Mondor (his real name was Philippe Girard) was the
brother of a more illustrious personage, the famous farce actor,
Tabarin, of whom Boileau was to write with such contempt in
the *Art poétique* where he laments the fact that in his comedies
Molière should too often have

> Quitté, pour le bouffon, l'agréable et le fin
> Et sans honte à Térence allié Tabarin.[1]

Both brothers are mentioned in another item in these accounts,
dated February 1619; Marie de Médicis orders her treasurer to
pay 'Philippe de Mondor, docteur en médecine, et Antoine
Girard, dit Tabarin, la somme de trois cents livres de laquelle
nous leur avons fait don tant en considération de ce qu'ils ont
représenté plusieurs comédies devant nous pour notre plaisir et
service que pour leur faire sentir notre libéralité.[2] It is obvious
that in the opening decades of the seventeenth century there
was not an unbridgeable gulf between the taste of the court and
that of the low-born spectators who applauded farce actors like
Gros-Guillaume and Tabarin, and that the public performances
given at the Hôtel de Bourgogne and at other places in Paris did
not provide an exclusively plebeian entertainment.

Fortunately we do not need to get involved in the contro-
versies concerning the social composition of theatre audiences
in the opening decades of the century for which, as for other
questions concerning the theatrical life of the period, solid information is sadly lacking. In contrast, for the decades of the century which concern us, the period from roughly 1630 to 1680
which saw the production of all but one of the masterpieces of

---

[1] *Œuvres complètes*, p.178.
[2] Bibliothèque nationale, Cinq Cents Colbert, vol. 92, ff. 187, 201, 214.

Corneille, Molière, and Racine, our knowledge is much less scrappy and is sufficient to give us a fairly clear idea of what sort of people frequented the public theatres of the capital.

It may well be that with the changes which took place in the theatrical world of Paris, roughly in the period 1625-35, audiences became rather less mixed than they had previously been. With two companies permanently installed in the capital and a new generation of playwrights supported by the patronage of great noblemen and above all Richelieu, the theatre became much more fashionable. For a time one continues to find references to the presence of plebeian spectators in the different Paris theatres. As late as 1663, in Molière's little play, *La Critique de l'École des femmes*, there is the famous reference to the presence of lackeys among the audience in his theatre. In making fun of the prudish reactions of some women spectators to *L'École des femmes*, one of the characters declares: 'Quelqu'un même des laquais cria tout haut qu'elles étaient plus chastes des oreilles que de tout le reste du corps.'[1] Indeed it seems that it was not until rather later that lackeys were banned by royal edict from attending the theatre.

It is true that the word *peuple* when applied to seventeenth-century theatre audiences can be highly ambiguous as in certain contexts it can mean simply 'audience, public', and sometimes, as in 'la cour et le peuple', it is used in a sense which obviously includes people who were very far from plebeian in the modern sense of the term.

None the less in the 1630s and 1640s there are clearly some occasions when the term *peuple* applied to part of the audience had a definitely plebeian meaning. In 1639 in his *Apologie du théâtre* Georges de Scudéry makes some extremely rude references to plebeian spectators in the *parterre* such as 'cette multitude ignorante que la farce attire à la comédie'.[2] At about the same time (although not published until 1657, his *Pratique du théâtre* was written much earlier) Abbé d'Aubignac speaks scathingly of the low tastes of the plebeian section of the audience:

. . . La populace, élevée dans la fange at entretenue de sentiments et de discours déshonnêtes, se trouve fort disposée à recevoir pour bonnes les

---

[1] Sc. 3.   [2] Paris, 1639, p. 89.

méchantes bouffonneries de nos farces, et prend toujours plaisir d'y voir les images de ce qu'elle a accoutumé de dire et de faire.[1]

Then there is the much quoted passage from Sorel's *La Maison des jeux*, published in 1642, in which he denounces the noisy *racaille* to be found among the spectators in the *parterre*:

Le parterre est fort incommode pour la presse qui s'y trouve de mille marauds mêlés parmi les honnêtes gens, auxquels ils veulent quelquefois faire des affronts, et ayant fait des querelles pour un rien, mettent la main à l'épée et interrompent toute la comédie. Dans leur plus parfait repos ils ne cessent aussi de parler, de siffler et de crier, et pource qu'ils n'ont rien payé à l'entrée et qu'ils ne viennent là qu'à faute d'autre occupation, ils ne se soucient guère d'entendre ce que disent les comédiens. C'est une preuve que la comédie est infâme, de ce qu'elle est fréquentée par de telles gens, et l'on montre que ceux qui ont la puissance dans le monde en font bien peu de cas, puisqu'ils n'empêchent point que toute cette racaille y entre sans payer, pour y faire du désordre.[2]

If we are to believe such witnesses, the audiences for which Corneille and his contemporaries catered in the 1630s still contained a noticeable plebeian element.

It is, however, significant that from the middle of the seventeenth century until the closing decades of the Ancien Régime one finds scarcely any references to the presence of such spectators. It is only from the 1760s onwards that writers begin to refer, naturally with scorn, to the gradual infiltration of plebeian spectators into theatres like the Comédie Française and the Théâtre Italien. In the hundred years or so before that date it would seem as if the cheapest part of the various Paris theatres, the *parterre*, was largely a middle-class preserve. Among the spectators in this part of the house about whose presence we have ample evidence were budding playwrights. Naturally once they had established themselves, they enjoyed the privilege of free admission and could choose a more comfortable way of seeing a play. We are told that Pierre Corneille—the 'vieux poète malintentionné' whom Racine refers to in his savage first preface to the play—sat in a box at the first performance of his younger rival's *Britannicus*,[3] but he himself refers in *La Suite du Menteur* to the presence of writers in the *parterre* applying the famous

---

[1] *La Pratique du théâtre*, pp. 74–5.
[2] Paris, 1642, 2 vols., vol. ii, pp. 424–5.
[3] Boursault, *Artémise et Poliante* (Paris, 1670), p. 3.

rules to other people's plays. In this comedy he makes the main character, Dorante, and his servant, Cliton, discuss putting their new adventures on the stage as in *Le Menteur*:

Cliton: Mais peut-on l'ajuster dans les vingt et quatre heures?
Dorante: Qu'importe?
Cliton: A mon avis, ce sont bien les meilleures;
      Car, grâces au bon Dieu, nous nous y connaissons;
      Les poètes au parterre en font tant de leçons,
      Et là cette science est si bien éclaircie
      Que nous savons que c'est que de péripétie,
      Catastase, épisode, unité, dénoûment,
      Et quand nous en parlons, nous parlons congrûment.[1]

Again one of the characters in Sorel's *Maison des jeux* replies to the criticisms of the spectators in the *parterre* which we have just quoted, pointing out that 'la plupart de nos poètes qui sont les plus capables de juger des pièces, n'y vont point ailleurs.[2]

It may be objected that this period saw too much poverty among writers, too many 'poètes crottés' to use the language of the time, for the presence of writers in the *parterre* to throw much light on its social composition and in particular to prove that it contained many solid bourgeois. Yet there is plenty of evidence that this was the case, so much so that it would take several pages to quote all of it; only a few examples can be given here. The expression 'le noble et le bourgeois' is frequently used in writings of the time as shorthand for the theatre audiences, as when Jean Loret in his rhymed news-sheet speaks of a tragedy being performed at Molière's theatre 'pour le noble et le bourgeois'.[3] 'Le bourgeois' is often mentioned in his own right as one of the pillars of the Paris theatres as in Loret's references to Molière's *Dom Juan* with its 'changements de théâtre/Dont le bourgeois est idolâtre',[4] or in Chappuzeau's statement that, since the royal edict of 1673 has put an end to disorders there, 'le bourgeois peut venir avec plus de plaisir à la comédie'[5] That the bourgeois mainly frequented the *parterre* is made clear in official documents such as that provided by d'Argenson, the *Lieutenant de police*, who speaks of the greater part of the large number of

---

[1] Act v, sc. 5.   [2] Vol. ii, p. 473.
[3] *La Muse historique*, ed. C. Livet (Paris, 1857–78, 4 vols.), vol. iii, p. 140.
[4] Ibid., vol. iv, p. 312.
[5] *Le Théâtre français*, p. 148.

spectators in the *parterre* of the Comédie Française one day in 1700 when disorders broke out there, as being 'gens de collège, de palais ou de commerce',[1] that is teachers, lawyers, and merchants. A vivid picture of the spectators on the stage contrasted with the bourgeois spectators in the *parterre* of the Théâtre Italien towards the end of the century is to be found in the final scene of Regnard and Dufresny's comedy, *Les Chinois*, performed in 1692:

Les Italiens donnent un champ libre sur la scène à tout le monde. L'officier vient jusques au bord du théâtre étaler impunément aux yeux du marchand la dorure qu'il lui doit encore. L'enfant de famille, sur les frontières de l'orchestre, fait la moue à l'usurier qui ne saurait lui demander ni le principal, ni les intérêts. Le fils, mêlé avec les acteurs, rit de voir son père avaricieux faire le pied de grue dans le parterre pour lui laisser quinze sols de plus après sa mort.

There is also in the literature of the time[2] an extraordinary number of references to the presence in the *parterre* of groups of 'marchands de la rue Saint-Denis'; these were not small shopkeepers, but prosperous retailers of luxury goods.

English travellers of the time who were men of some social position made no difficulty about standing in the cheapest part of the Paris theatres which they frequented. In 1664 Edward Browne, the son of Sir Thomas Browne, the author of *Religio Medici*, visited Paris as part of his grand tour. At this time he was only twenty-two; he was in due course to follow in his father's footsteps and become a doctor. When he went to the Palais Royal to see a performance by Molière's company, he felt no compunction about buying a ticket to stand in the *parterre*: 'In the afternoon I heard a Comedy at Palais-Royal. They were Monseir's Comedians; they had a farce after it. I gave Quinze Solz to stand upon the grounde. The name of it was *Coeur de Mari*.[3] They were not to be compared with the Londoners.'[4] Two years later Philip Skippon, the son of Cromwell's Major-General, a young Cambridge graduate who not long afterwards

[1] *Notes*, ed. L. Larchey and E. Mabille (Paris, 1866), p. 20.

[2] See Donneau de Vise, *Zélinde*, sc. 3; Abbé d'Aubignac, *Deux dissertations sur les tragédies de M. Corneille*, pp. 18-29, and *Quatrième dissertation*, p. 184; G. Guéret, *Le Parnasse réformé*, p. 83; Boursault, *Artémise et Poliante*, p. 3.

[3] *L'Ecole des maris*, followed by 'la farce de la Casaque' according to La Grange's register for this date (p. 67).

[4] *A Journal of a Visit to Paris in the year 1664*, ed. G. Keynes (London, 1923), p. 16.

was to become an M.P. and a knight, saw both the Italian actors and Molière's company perform at the Palais Royal, and once again neither he nor his companion (or companions) made any difficulty about standing in the *parterre*:

Palais Cardinal is a fair palace with handsome walks. Here Madame Henrietta, the duchess of Orleans, lives. At one side of this house is a public stage where the Italian and French comedians act by turns. I saw here *Il marîtaggion d'una Statua*, a merry play where the famous buffoon Scaramuccio, acted. Three antick dances pleased the spectators. The *Quatre Scaramuccie* was another pleasant Italian comedy. We stood in the parterre, or pit, and paid 30 sols apiece for seeing the first, and but 15 sols for the last.

We saw a French comedy entitled *L'estourdye* which was better acted than we expected. We paid for seeing this, and standing in the pit, 15 sols a man.[1]

Nor did a French nobleman disdain to stand in the *parterre* if he went to the theatre on his own or in male company. It is true that we chiefly learn of the presence of such spectators in that part of the house when they were drunk and created a disturbance, but presumably they also frequented it when they were sober.

The spectators in the *parterre* were certainly not always well behaved. We know from unimpeachable documents that twice during the last few months of Molière's life there were disorders in his theatre. On Sunday, 9 October 1672, during a performance of *La Comtesse d'Escarbagnas* and *L'Amour médecin* 'plusieurs gens de livrée et autres firent insulte à un homme d'épée auquel ils donnèrent quantité de coups de bâton desquels il est grièvement blessé, et même jetèrent plusieurs pierres aux acteurs qui jouaient la comédie.'[2] While Molière himself was on the stage, 'il fut jeté du parterre le gros bout d'une pipe à fumer sur le théâtre'.[3] Witnesses who gave evidence about the incident all agreed that the culprits were pages; their victim, described as 'un homme d'épée', might or might not have been an officer.

On 13 January 1673, just over a month before Molière's death, further disorders took place at the Palais Royal during a performance of the highly successful *tragédie-ballet, Psyché*, which he had composed with the assistance of Pierre Corneille

[1] *An Account of a Journey through Part of the Low Countries, Germany, Italy and France,* in *A Collection of Voyages and Travels* (London, 1732), vol. vi, p. 731.
[2] E. Campardon, *Documents inédits sur J.B.Poquelin Molière* (Paris, 1871), pp. 31-2.
[3] Ibid., p. 34.

and Quinault. A *commissaire au Châtelet* was fetched to the theatre by the news that 'dans le parterre il y avait quantité de gens d'épée entrés sous prétexte d'entendre la comédie . . . lesquels composaient entre eux, contre la volonté de sadite Majesté, . . . un désordre et une sédition comme il a été ci-devant fait à l'Hôtel de Bourgogne'.[1] The *commissaire* went on to the stage,

d'où aussitôt que la première entrée s'est faite, avons aperçu dans ledit parterre, à la faveur de la clarté des chandelles, quelques gens d'épée à nous inconnus qui se seraient approchés dudit théâtre, lesquels murmuraient et frappaient du pied à terre, et quand la machine de Vénus est descendue, le chœur des chanteurs de cette entrée récitant tous ensemble *Descendez, mère des Amours!* lesdits gens d'épée, autant que nous avons pu remarquer être au nombre de vingt-cinq ou trente, de complot, auraient troublé lesdits chanteurs par des hurlements, chansons dérisionnaires et frappements de pied dans le parterre et contre les ais de l'enclos où sont les joueurs d'instruments.[2]

The uproar caused by these rowdies finally brought the performance to an end; they were offered their money back, but they refused and demanded instead that the play should start all over again. When this was done, they apparently behaved themselves; at least the *commissaire*'s report breaks off at this point.

Once again we have no means of telling what was the rank of these 'gens d'épée', but if this was conduct unworthy of an officer and a gentleman, we cannot necessarily conclude that they were 'other ranks'. At the Comédie Française in 1691 a performance of *La Devineresse*, the *pièce à machines* of De Visé and Thomas Corneille, was brought to an end by the disorders created by a gang of rowdies, led by a drunken officer with the delightful name of Sallo. This officer, 'capitaine au régiment de Champagne', the documents in the case relate, 'força la garde et entra dans le parterre', followed by other members of his company. Sallo then climbed up on to the stage from the *parterre* and shouted: 'Connais-tu ce bougre qui est à la porte de la Comédie? Je lui viens de foutre un bon coup d'épée dans le ventre. Je suis un capitaine qui ai vingt amis dans le parterre.'[3]

Despite successive royal edicts trouble continued from this quarter to the end of the century. In November 1700 the

[1] Ibid., p. 66.   [2] Ibid., pp. 68–9.
[3] E. Campardon, *Les Comédiens du Roi de la Troupe française,* pp. 290–7.

Lieutenant de police, d'Argenson, describes the following incident at the Comédie Française in which a *mousquetaire* was involved:

Avant-hier il arriva du bruit à la Comédie, à l'occasion d'un chien danois que M. le marquis de Livry, le fils, y avait mené. Ce chien se mit à faire le manège sur le théâtre et à faire voir son agilité en cent manières différentes. Messieurs du parterre firent pour l'encourager tous les bruits de chasse dont chacun put s'aviser, et l'un de ceux qui affecta le plus de s'y distinguer, ce fut le sieur de Creil, mousquetaire de la seconde compagnie, fort sujet à troubler la tranquillité du spectacle, aimant le désordre et l'excitant en toute rencontre, également prompt à critiquer et à applaudir, pourvu que ce soit avec éclat et qui regrette fort le temps des sifflets.[1]

However, the presence of officers in this part of the house was by no means always unwelcome to the actors of the different theatres; their absence was lamented when in wartime they had to return to the front with the opening of the campaigning season in the spring. In Dufresny's *Départ des comédiens*, a little comedy performed at the Théâtre Italien in 1694, Arlequin laments the fact that at this season of the year 'il n'est officier qui ne parte' and that spring 'dépeuple de plumets théâtres et ruelles'. He goes on:

> Qu'êtes-vous devenus, jeunes foudres de guerre,
> Qui triomphiez jadis dans ce vaste parterre?
>   Hélas! je n'y vois plus
>   Ce doux flux et reflux
>   De têtes ondoyantes,
> Qui rend en plein hiver nos moissons abondantes,
> Quand le troupeau guerrier et terrestre et marin
>   Vient piétiner notre terrain;
>   En y semant quelques paroles,
>   Nous recueillons force pistoles . . .[2]

Thus if the *parterre* appears to have been largely the preserve of the middle classes, of merchants and professional men, including writers and aspiring writers, it also contained at least a sprinkling of noblemen, drunk or sober.

---

[1] *Notes*, p. 41. 'Le temps des sifflets' is a reference to the craze in the 1690s for interrupting performances in the Paris theatres with an instrument of that name. A master butcher who had never been to the theatre before spent three weeks in prison for having committed this offence; he stated in the petition for his release that 'l'exposant se servit d'un instrument avec lequel il éveille ses garçons le matin' (Tralage, *Recueil*, vol. iv, f. 171.
[2] Sc. 1.

There is no question but that the all male spectators in this part of the theatre had a considerable influence. Thanks to the register kept by Hubert for the last year of the existence of Molière's theatre, we know that at 113 out of 131 performances more than half the spectators stood in the *parterre*. It is true that both in Molière's theatre and at the Comédie Française from 1680 the custom of doubling prices in the *parterre* during the opening performances of a new play tended to reduce the number of tickets sold for that part of the house, but under ordinary conditions these spectators formed a majority among the audience whenever older plays were revived and during the first run of new plays as soon as prices for the *parterre* had been reduced to normal. Clearly such spectators were extremely important from the numerical point of view, and even though the proportion of the audience which they represented generally fell during the opening performances of new plays, these were mostly well attended and on such occasions there could be at least three or four hundred spectators in the *parterre*. This mass of men, packed together like sardines, was obviously in a position to express its reactions in a way which could have a considerable effect on the fate of the play.

At any rate from the 1660s onwards, we continually find most flattering references to the good taste of the *parterre*. Molière's *Critique de l'École des femmes* (1663) furnishes the first example of such praise; here we see the actor-manager who knew on which side his bread was buttered and was very conscious of the fact that the spectators who bought tickets for the *parterre* generally represented more than half his audience. His spokesman, Dorante, makes a vigorous defence of the taste of the spectators in this part of the theatre when he rebukes the Marquis for his contemptuous attitude towards them:

Apprends, Marquis, je te prie, et les autres aussi, que le bon sens n'a point de place déterminée à la comédie; que la différence du demi-louis d'or[1] et de la pièce de quinze sols[2] ne fait rien du tout au bon goût; que debout ou assis, on peut donner un mauvais jugement; et qu'enfin, à le prendre en général, je me fierais assez à l'approbation du parterre, par la raison qu'entre ceux qui le composent, il y en a plusieurs[3] qui sont capables de juger d'une

---

[1] 5½ livres, the price of a ticket to the *premières loges* or a seat on the stage.
[2] The price of a ticket to the *parterre* (20 sous=1 livre).
[3] 'Beaucoup, quantité, grand nombre' (*Dictionnaire de l'Académie française*, 1694).

pièce selon les règles, et que les autres en jugent par la bonne façon d'en juger, qui est de se laisser prendre aux choses, et de n'avoir ni prévention aveugle, ni complaisance affectée, ni délicatesse ridicule.[1]

Flattery of the *parterre* is carried much further in *Les Chinois*, the comedy written by Regnard and Dufresny for the Théâtre Italien. In the last scene the *Parterre* enters to act as judge in the debate between Colombine, representing the Théâtre Italien, and Arlequin, who represents the Comédie Française. Arlequin is made to greet the arrival of the *Parterre* with the words: 'Malepeste! il faut ouvrir la porte à deux battants, c'est notre père nourricier. Qu'il entre, en payant, s'entend.' The *Parterre* puts forward sweeping claims as to its function in the theatre: 'Ne savez-vous pas que je suis seul juge naturel, et en dernier ressort, des comédiens et des comédies? Voilà avec quoi je prononce mes arrêts (*Il donne un coup de sifflet*).'[2] When Colombine speaks of 'son Excellence, Monseigneur le Parterre', Arlequin protests at such flattery, but she retorts with comic enthusiasm:

Non, ce n'est point la flatterie qui me dénoue la langue; je rends simplement les hommages dus à ce souverain plénipotentiaire. C'est l'éperon des auteurs, le frein des comédiens, l'inspecteur et curieux examinateur des hautes et basses loges, et de tout ce qui se passe en icelles; en un mot, c'est un juge incorruptible, qui, bien loin de prendre de l'argent pour juger, commence par en donner à la porte de l'audience.

When the *Parterre* finally gives its judgement, Arlequin exclaims in horror: 'O tempora! O mores! J'appelle de ce jugement-là aux loges', to which the former replies: 'Mon jugement est sans appel.'

No doubt it would be very unwise to take all this literally; one must bear in mind the effect which such paradoxes must have had on theatre audiences drawn from the profoundly aristocratic society which existed in France in the reign of Louis XIV. Given the prevailing worship of rank and social position, it was inevitable that the outlook and ideals of the aristocracy should exercise a considerable influence on the drama of the age. The section of the nobility which gravitated around the king in Paris and later at Versailles was powerfully represented in the different theatres which served Paris in the course of the seventeenth century. There was clearly a considerable overlap between the

---

[1] Sc. 5.   [2] See above, p.89 no.1.

audiences present at court performances and those to be found in the public theatres.

It is obvious that the more expensive seats in these theatres were occupied by persons of rank or wealth. Theatre prices rose fairly steeply in the course of the century for all sorts of reasons, including taxes; a ticket to the *parterre* at the Hôtel de Bour-gogne cost a mere 5 sous at the beginning of the century com-pared with 18 at the Comédie Française at the end of the reign of Louis XIV. Although numerically the *parterre* might be extemely important, its contribution to the total box-office receipts was much smaller than its numbers might at first suggest. This is particularly striking in Molière's theatre as there the best seats, those in the first row of boxes and on the stage, were very expensive. The result was that, to take the example of the first performance of *Le Malade imaginaire* in 1673, while 394 out of the 682 spectators stood in the *parterre*, tickets for that part of the theatre, even with prices doubled, accounted for less than a third of the total receipts—591 livres out of 1,892. In contrast seats on the stage and in the *premières loges* contributed more to the total—682 livres.

At the Comédie Française the charges made for the best seats in the theatre were proportionately less heavy in relation to the cost of tickets to the *parterre* than they had been in Molière's theatre. Even so, despite the large numbers of spectators present in the *parterre* on most occasions, their contribution to the total receipts of the performance fell well below 50 per cent, and could even fall as low as a quarter. Thus even if the society of the time had not accorded the respect which it did to birth and money, the men and women of blue blood and wealth who sat in the first row of boxes or on the stage had an importance, from the financial point of view, which far outweighed their numbers, and, of course, both actors and actresses did bestow upon the upper classes of the society of their age the respect which the prevailing social outlook demanded.

If the ladies of the aristocracy, with their male escorts, chiefly frequented the *premières loges*, another part of the theatre which sometimes counted among its spectators illustri-ous personages of both sexes was the *amphithéâtre*, the rows of seats facing the stage at the far end of the *parterre*. Thus in

December 1672 Louis XIV's brother, Monsieur, accompanied on one occasion by his second wife, the German princess Charlotte Elizabeth, was twice present at performances of *Psyché* at Molière's theatre and occupied with his suit 'deux bancs de l'amphithéâtre'. The other part of the theatre which contained a high proportion of aristocrats—this time men only[1]—was the stage. While on occasion the number of these spectators could be quite small, there were times when they were so numerous that it is difficult to imagine how both they and the actors were accommodated on the stage. On one occasion in the last year of the life of Molière's company there were as many as thirty-six, while the registers of the Comédie Française record for its first performance in 1680 as many as 150.[2] Writers—Corneille and Molière among others—are shown by contemporary documents to have gone on occasion to this part of the house, but it seems mainly to have been frequented by the young bloods of the aristocracy.

For a vivid, if naturally somewhat exaggerated picture of the behaviour of the aristocratic fops of the time when they sat on the stage, we need only turn to the famous description given by one of the characters in Molière's *Les Fâcheux* (1661):

> J'étais sur le théâtre, en humeur d'écouter
> La pièce, qu'à plusieurs j'avais ouï vanter;
> Les acteurs commençaient, chacun prêtait silence,
> Lorsque d'un air bruyant et plein d'extravagance,
> Un homme à grands canons[3] est entré brusquement,
> En criant: 'Holà ho! un siège promptement!'
> Et de son grand fracas surprenant l'assemblée,
> Dans le plus bel endroit a la pièce troublée ...
> Tandis que là-dessus je haussais les épaules,
> Les acteurs ont voulu continuer leurs rôles;
> Mais l'homme pour s'asseoir a fait nouveau fracas,

---

[1] When Abbé Boyer's biblical tragedy, *Judith*, was performed at the Comédie Française during Lent in 1695, it had a very successful first run and was particularly popular with women. According to Lesage 'c'était tous les jours une si grande affluence de femmes de toutes sortes de conditions qu'on ne savait où les placer. Les hommes furent obligés de leur céder le théâtre et de se tenir debout dans les coulisses. Quelle fureur! Imaginez-vous deux cents femmes assises sur des banquettes où l'on ne voit ordinairement que des hommes, et tenant des mouchoirs étalés sur leurs genoux pour essuyer leurs yeux dans les endroits touchants' (quoted in C. and F. Parfaict, *Histoire du théâtre français*, vol. xiv, p. 408).

[2] *Le Registre d'Hubert*, p. 110; Chevalley, *Album Théâtre classique*, p. 214.

[3] See above, p. 31 n. 2.

Et traversant encor le théâtre à grands pas,
Bien que dans les côtés il pût être à son aise,
Au milieu du devant il a planté sa chaise,
Et de son large dos morguant les spectateurs
Aux trois quarts du parterre a caché les acteurs.
Un bruit s'est élevé, dont un autre eût eu honte;
Mais lui, ferme et constant, n'en a fait aucun compte,
Et se serait tenu comme il s'était posé,
Si, pour mon infortune, il ne m'eût avisé.
'Ha! Marquis, m'a-t-il dit, prenant près de moi place,
Comment te portes-tu? Souffre que je t'embrasse.'
Au visage sur l'heure un rouge m'est monté
Que l'on me vît connu d'un tel éventé . . .
Il m'a fait à l'abord cent questions frivoles,
Plus haut que les acteurs élevant ses paroles.
Chacun le maudissait; et moi, pour l'arrêter:
'Je serais, ai-je dit, bien aise d'écouter.
—Tu n'as point vu ceci, Marquis? Ah! Dieu me damne,
Je le trouve assez drôle, et je n'y suis pas âne;
Je sais par quelles lois un ouvrage est parfait;
Et Corneille me vient lire tout ce qu'il fait.'
Là-dessus de la pièce il m'a fait un sommaire,
Scène à scène averti de ce qui s'allait faire;
Et jusques à des vers qu'il en savait par cœur,
Il me les récitait tout haut avant l'acteur.
J'avais beau m'en défendre, il a poussé sa chance,
Et s'est devers la fin levé longtemps d'avance;
Car les gens du bel air, pour agir galamment,
Se gardent bien surtout d'ouïr le dénouement.[1]

It is a pity that neither Molière nor any other writer of the time left behind an equally vivid, if caricatural, picture of other sections of the seventeenth-century theatre audience, particularly of the ladies and their male escorts in the *premières loges*.

The importance of the aristocratic section of that audience is well illustrated by Molière's *Critique de l'École des femmes*. First, (and this example was to be followed slavishly by later writers who produced a little play of this kind in defence of their comedies) with the exception of the jealous playwright, Lysidas, all the characters who assemble in a Paris *salon* and argue over the merits of *L'École des femmes* are drawn from the aristocracy. What is more, if Molière puts into the mouth of Dorante a defence of the taste of the *parterre*, the same

[1] Act I, sc. 1.

character delivers an eloquent eulogy of the taste of the court
in answer to the sneers of the bourgeois writer:

Achevez, Monsieur Lysidas. Je vois bien que vous voulez dire que la cour
ne se connaît pas à ces choses; et c'est le refuge ordinaire de vous autres,
Messieurs les auteurs, dans le mauvais succès de vos ouvrages, que d'accuser
l'injustice du siècle et le peu de lumière des courtisans. Sachez, s'il vous
plaît, Monsieur Lysidas, que les courtisans ont d'aussi bons yeux que
d'autres; qu'on peut être habile avec un point de Venise et des plumes,
aussi bien qu'avec une perruque courte et un petit rabat uni;[1] que la grande
épreuve de toutes vos comédies, c'est le jugement de la cour; que c'est son
goût qu'il faut étudier pour trouver l'art de réussir; qu'il n'y a point de
lieu où les décisions soient si justes; et sans mettre en ligne de compte tous
les gens savants qui y sont, que, du simple bon sens naturel et du commerce
de tout le beau monde, on s'y fait une manière d'esprit, qui sans comparai-
son juge plus finement des choses que tout le savoir enrouillé des pédants.[2]

This reference to the presence of 'gens savants' at the court is
rather surprising. In contrast, in his *Épître à M. Racine* (1677),
Boileau describes in vivid terms the obstacles which Molière had
to overcome in his struggle for recognition, and he gives a far
from flattering account of the hostility shown by certain members of the nobility, both male and female, to his masterpieces:

> L'ignorance et l'erreur à ses naissantes pièces,
> En habits de marquis, en robes de comtesses,
> Venaient pour diffamer son chef-d'œuvre nouveau,
> Et secouaient la tête à l'endroit le plus beau.
> Le commandeur voulait la scène plus exacte;
> Le vicomte indigné sortait au second acte:
> L'un, défenseur zélé des bigots[3] mis en jeu,
> Pour prix de ses bons mots le condamnait au feu.
> L'autre, fougueux marquis, lui déclarant la guerre,
> Voulait venger la cour immolée au parterre.[4]

This passage also underlines the importance of the aristocratic
section of the theatre audiences of the time.

There is certainly no evidence that Louis XIV and his courtiers
showed any particular discernment in their choice of plays to be
performed in the various royal palaces. During Molière's lifetime
Les Fâcheux appears to have been the play of his most often

---

[1] Features of the dress of the nobleman compared with that of the bourgeois writer.
[2] Sc. 6. See also Clitandre's speech in Act iv, Sc. 3 of *Les Femmes savantes*.
[3] *Bigot* is defined as 'hypocrite, faux dévot' in the 1694 edition of the *Dictionnaire
de l'Académie française*; Boileau is obviously referring to the *Tartuffe* controversy.
[4] *Œuvres complètes*, p. 127.

given at court, and there is no evidence that he ever performed *Le Misanthrope* there. However, to conclude that in its dealings with the theatre the aristocracy did not exhibit any particular refinement of taste is not to deny that it exercised an influence on drama commensurate with its exalted place in the society of the day. The ladies and their male escorts in the more expensive boxes and the noblemen sitting or standing on the stage did play an important part in moulding the taste of the day in the theatre as in other forms of literature. Although middle-class and even for a time plebeian spectators were undoubtedly present among the audiences of the capital, given the social structure of seventeenth-century France, the upper classes, from the princes of the blood and the *grands seigneurs* and their womenfolk downwards, exercised an influence on drama which was out of proportion to the fairly considerable numbers which they furnished to the theatre audiences of the time.

Mixed as the audiences in the public theatre undoubtedly were, from the point of view of social composition, in sheer numbers they none the less represented a small élite. It is true that it is only for the last year of Molière's career in Paris that, thanks to the *Registre d'Hubert*, we can calculate for the first time how many spectators paid to see his company perform in the course of the theatrical year. In considering these figures, we have to bear in mind that Paris probably had a population of some half a million, one which was temporarily swollen by visitors from the provinces and from further afield, some of whom, as we know from their letters and diaries, frequented the theatres of the capital. In the theatrical year 1672/73 Molière's company performed 131 times and attracted some 52,000 spectators—an average daily attendance of 400.

Thanks to the summary of the registers of the Comédie Française produced by the late Carrington Lancaster,[1] we can work out how many spectators paid for admission to this theatre from 1680 onwards. In attempting to interpret these figures we have to bear in mind that whereas Molière's company had to compete with several others, the Comédie Française had as its only rivals the Opéra and the Théâtre Italien, and that after the

[1] *The Comédie Française, 1680–1701: Plays, Actors, Spectators, Finances* (Baltimore, 1941).

expulsion of the Italian actors in 1697, it was the only Paris theatre putting on straight plays. The total number of spectators fluctuated fairly violently from year to year, reaching in 1698/99 193,000, an exceptionally high figure, and falling as low as 109,000 in 1683/84. The average—nearly 140,000—looks at first sight very impressive until one does a little arithmetic. There is evidence that a small number of people went very frequently to the theatre, seeing a successful new play more than once and also being assiduous in their attendance at revivals. Thus a thousand people attending the Comédie Française fifty times in a year could account for over a third of this total, and two thousand more going twenty times a year could account for another 40,000 attendances; these three thousand people could leave only some 50,000 attendances for those spectators who went only once in the year or else very infrequently.

All this is, of course, only playing with figures in an orgy of guesswork. Where we are on firmer ground in trying to assess the size of theatre audiences in the Paris of our period is by finding out how large was the number of spectators which the average successful play attracted during its first run; this gives us a rough idea of how many people were in the habit of attending the Comédie Française. In the period from 1680 to 1700 Boursault's five-act comedy, *Les Fables d'Ésope*, with the quite exceptional number of 43 performances attracted over 25,000 paying spectators, while a one-act play of Dancourt, *Les Vendages de Suresnes*, had 49 performances with over 33,000 spectators paying for admission. Clearly both these plays had such a vogue as to draw in people who did not normally go to the Comédie Française. If we examine the fate of other new plays put on in the same period we find that 10,000–12,000 people represented the largest number of spectators who could be expected to support a new play unless it enjoyed a great vogue, when the total attendance would reach from 15,000 to 17,000. In other words at the end of the seventeenth-century the number of regular patrons of the Comédie Française lay somewhere between a minimum of 10,000 and a maximum of 17,000.

We may conclude then that the theatre-going public of Paris in the Classical age of French drama was numerically a severely restricted one, given the population of the capital and its attractions for provincials and foreigners. The short run enjoyed by even the most successful plays of the period makes this point clear enough. Socially that audience appears to have been much more mixed than has sometimes been suggested. Certainly the middle classes were strongly represented there, and as late as the 1630s and 1640s there was probably a sprinkling of plebeian spectators. On the other hand the more aristocratic sections of society—so important in the France of Louis XIII and Louis XIV—also formed a considerable section of the audiences in the public theatres of the time, and it is their outlook rather than that of the middle layers of society which is most clearly reflected in the drama of the age. Lip-service is paid by many playwrights of the period to the importance of pleasing the *savants* and conforming to their rules, but in their franker moments they recognize that, in order to be successful, a play must appeal to a wider circle, to 'les honnêtes gens', few of whom (especially the ladies) could claim to be learned. Thus the drama of the age was strongly influenced by the aristocratic outlook of the society in which it was produced. It was certainly not a learned drama, written to please a tiny group of scholars and critics; indeed, especially in comedy and farce, it contains a down-to-earth element which, though attributed by Boileau amongst others to the influence of the lower and middle sections of society, suited equally well the not too squeamish or refined taste of the aristocratic spectators, both male and female.

v The rules

The contrast between French drama of the period from 1630 onwards and seventeenth-century English drama is well brought out by Samuel Chappuzeau in his one and only reference to the theatres of London: 'Les Anglais sont très bons comédiens pour leur nation; ils ont de fort beaux théâtres et des habits magnifiques, mais ni eux ni leurs poètes ne se piquent pas fort de s'attacher aux règles de la poétique, et dans une tragédie ils feront rire et pleurer, ce qui ne se peut souffrir en France, où l'on veut de la régularité.'[1] If at the beginning of the century there had been no such gap between English and French drama, in the 1630s and 1640s a number of theorists, known as 'les savants' or 'les doctes', had succeeded in establishing certain rules and in persuading both playwrights and the theatre-going public to accept them; this transformed French drama and cast it in a mould which was not to be finally broken until the Romantic revolution of the 1820s.

The most important of these theorists who based themselves on Aristotle and on writers, both French and foreign, who had produced since the Renaissance commentaries on his *Poetics*, was probably Abbé d'Aubignac. His *La Pratique du théâtre* which, though not published until 1657, was probably written around 1640, is, as its title idicates, concerned with the realities of the theatre of his day. It is a much more interesting work than the earlier treatise of a doctor named La Mesnardière, his *La Poétique*, published in 1639, as this follows very closely Aristotle and the writings of his learned commentators. In this same year there appeared as a preface to a play of Scudéry a fairly slight essay of a young writer named Sarasin, his *Discours de la tragédie*. Perhaps the most influential of these critics, partly through the newly formed Académie Française and the *salons* of the capital, was Jean Chapelain. As early as 1630 he produced

[1] *Le Théâtre français,* pp. 49–50.

his famous *Lettre sur la règle des vingt-quatre heures*; it was he who, seven years later, was to draw up the *Sentiments de l'Académie française sur le 'Cid'*.

The great playwrights of the age left behind very variable amounts of theoretical writings. Corneille wrote far more than Racine who can be said to have virtually confined himself to the prefaces of his plays. Though they are often interesting, especially those of *Britannicus* and *Bérénice*, they can scarcely be said to satisfy our curiosity. Corneille was much more generous in supplying us with information about his conception of drama. In addition to his prefaces he also produced for the 1660 edition of his *Théâtre* an *examen* for each of his plays; in these, looking back on his earlier works, he discusses them in the light of the now accepted rules. For each of the three volumes of this edition he also wrote a separate *discours*—*Discours de l'utilité et des parties du poème dramatique, Discours de la tragédie et des moyens de la traiter selon le vraisemblable ou le nécessaire,* and *Discours des trois unités d'action, de jour et de lieu*. In these essays, normally known for short as *Discours sur le poème dramatique*, he discusses the rules governing the various forms of drama, attempting frequently to bend them somewhat to suit his own particular practice as a playwright. Molière's views on comedy are occasionally to be found in his prefaces, but the most useful account of them is given in *La Critique de l'École des femmes*. Although *L'Impromptu de Versailles*, the other one-act play which he produced in the controversy stirred up by the success of *L'École des femmes*, is more concerned with acting, it also contains some points of literary interest.

Every sixth former knows that the Three Unities—those of time, place, and action—are the hallmark of a French Classical tragedy. This is true up to a point, at any rate in the sense that by this criterion one can clearly differentiate between a Classical tragedy and, say, a *drame romantique* or an Elizabethan tragedy. It is the case that a thorough-going French Classical tragedy must have only one action, that is to say all the sub-plots must be incapable of being suppressed without rendering the main action inexplicable, and both the main plot and the sub-plots must arise out of the data supplied in the exposition. Again, all the action must take place at one particular spot and must not last longer than twenty-four hours. Indeed for some of the theorists of the period ideally the action should last the same length of time as the performance with a slight extension for the action taking place in the intervals between the acts.

The rule of the Three Unities was recapitulated very clearly in some well-known lines in Boileau's *Art poétique* in which he skilfully blends didacticism and satire:

> Que le lieu de la scène y soit fixe et marqué.
> Un rimeur, sans péril, delà les Pyrénées
> Sur la scène en un jour renferme des années.
> Là souvent le héros d'un spectacle grossier,
> Enfant au premier acte, est barbon au dernier.
> Mais nous, que la raison à ses règles engage,
> Nous voulons qu'avec art l'action se ménage:
> Qu'en un lieu, qu'en un jour, un seul fait accompli
> Tienne jusqu'à la fin le théâtre rempli.[1]

In the final couplet Boileau goes rather too far in speaking of 'un seul fait'; the theorists were not quite as restrictive as this. D'Aubignac, for instance, makes an obvious point when he writes: 'Il n'y a point d'action humaine toute simple et qui ne soit soutenue de plusieurs autres qui la précèdent, qui l'accompagnent, qui la suivent, et qui toutes ensemble la composent et lui donnent l'être.'[2]

This rule gave rise to considerable controversy round about the crucial year 1630. This opened, so far as published documents go, with the defiant preface which a certain François Ogier wrote in 1628 for a friend's tragicomedy. Whom he was attacking when he thus defends the position of those playwrights who reject the rules is something of a mystery, but the preface is certainly an interesting document. Ogier criticizes the rule of unity of time—the one which aroused most controversy[3]—as destroying the pleasure of the spectator:

La poésie, et particulièrement celle qui est composée pour le théâtre, n'est faite que pour le plaisir et le divertissement, et ce plaisir ne peut procéder que de la variété des événements qui s'y représentent, lesquels ne pouvant

---

[1] *Œuvres complètes*, p. 170.   [2] *La Pratique du théâtre*, p. 87.
[3] In his *Poetics* Aristotle lays down no rule, but merely states that tragedy endeavours, as far as possible, to confine itself to a single revolution of the sun, or only slightly to exceed this limit. He says nothing about unity of place.

pas se rencontrer facilement dans le cours d'une journée, les poètes ont été contraints de quitter peu à peu la pratique des premiers qui s'étaient resserrés dans des bornes trop étroites.[1]

He even goes so far as to criticize one of the main principles of French Classicism, the imitation of the Ancients. While professing due respect for the Greeks, he declares that it is useless to point to their example and to imitate them slavishly. That is not the way to create great works since the taste of every nation is different: 'Les Grecs ont travaillé pour la Grèce, et ont réussi au jugement des honnêtes gens de leur temps, et nous les imiterons bien mieux si nous donnons quelque chose au génie de notre pays et au goût de notre langue, que non pas en nous obligeant de suivre pas à pas et leur invention et leur élocution, comme ont fait quelques-uns des nôtres.'[2] The Ancients, he maintains, land themselves in two serious difficulties in their striving to observe unity of time; they crowd too many events into the short space of twenty-four hours or less and are 'contraints d'introduire à chaque bout de champ des messagers pour raconter les choses qui se sont passées les jours précédents, et les motifs des actions qui se font pour l'heure sur le théâtre'.[3]

These criticisms remind one of the complaint of the lack of physical action on the stage which Victor Hugo brought against Classical tragedy almost exactly two hundred years later in the *Préface du Cromwell*: 'Nous ne voyons en quelque sorte sur le théâtre que les coudes de l'action; ses mains sont ailleurs.'[4] Again, when Hugo speaks of 'le drame, qui fond sous un même souffle le grotesque et le sublime, le terrible et le bouffon, la tragédie et la comédie',[5] we are reminded of the well-known passage in Ogier's preface in which he defends the mingling of the comic and the tragic which was to be utterly banned by seventeenth-century dramatic theorists:

Car de dire qu'il est malséant de faire paraître en une même pièce les mêmes personnes, traitant tantôt d'affaires sérieuses, importantes et tragiques, et incontinent après de choses communes, vaines et comiques, c'est ignorer la

---

[1] Jean de Schelandre, *Tyr et Sidon, tragédie, et Tyr et Sidon, tragi-comédie,* ed. J.W. Barker (Paris, 1975), p.153.
[2] p.157.   [3] p.153.
[4] *Théâtre complet,* ed. R. Purnal et al. (Paris, 1967–9, 2 vols.), vol.i, p.428.
[5] Ibid., vol.i, p.422.

condition de la vie des hommes, de qui les jours et les heures sont bien souvent entrecoupés de ris et de larmes, de contentement et d'affliction, selon qu'ils sont agités de la bonne ou de la mauvaise fortune.[1]

Whoever the supporters of the unities whom Ogier was attacking may have been, it is certain that Jean Chapelain was prominent among them. In November 1630, in reply to a letter setting forth objections to this rule, he composed his *Lettre sur la règle des vingt-quatre heures*. From his starting-point that the aim of poetry is imitation and that this imitation must be so perfect 'qu'il ne paraisse aucune différence entre la chose imitée et celle qui imite',[2] he proceeds to argue that if the action of a play is carried beyond twenty-four hours, the spectators cease to find the result credible:

. . . L'œil des spectateurs se trouvant surchargé d'objets, et se laissant persuader avec peine que pendant trois heures qu'il a employées au spectacle il se soit passé des mois et des années, l'esprit qui juge sur le tout, reconnaissant qu'il y a de l'impossibilité, et que par conséquent il donne de l'attention à une chose fausse, se relâche pour tout ce qu'il y peut avoir d'utile au reste, et ne souffre point l'impression sans laquelle tout le travail du poète est vain.[3]

Moreover, Chapelain rejects explicitly Ogier's claim that the more events a play contains, the greater is the spectator's pleasure. 'Je nie', he declares, 'que le meilleur poème dramatique soit celui qui embrasse le plus d'actions, et dis au contraire qu'il n'en doit contenir qu'une et qu'il ne la faut encore que de bien médiocre longueur.'[4] Chapelain, it should be added, regards twenty-four hours as the extreme limit of time allowed to the playwright; normally the action should take place between sunrise and sunset of the same day. Besides, he argues, if an action lasting several years is brought on to the stage, it becomes impossible to observe unity of place since 'la longueur du temps porte avec soi une inévitable nécessité de plus d'un lieu.'[5]

Another important document in the history of the establishment of the unities is the preface which in 1631 a young playwright of Corneille's generation, Jean Mairet, attached to his

---

[1] Schelandre, *Tyr et Sidon,* p. 159.
[2] *Opuscules critiques*, ed. A. C. Hunter (Paris, 1936), p. 115.
[3] Ibid., p. 119.   [4] Ibid., p. 120.
[5] Ibid., p. 123.

tragi-comédie pastorale, La Silvanire. Here he explains how he had been encouraged by two noblemen to write a pastoral play 'avec toutes les rigueurs que les Italiens ont accoutumé de pratiquer en cet agréable genre d'écrire' and how he had discovered 'qu'ils n'avaient point eu de plus grand secret que de prendre leurs mesures sur celles des anciens Grecs et Latins, dont ils ont observé les règles plus religieusement que nous n'avons pas fait jusqu'ici'.[1] He expresses his surprise that the playwrights of his day should have ignored the rule of unity of time and consequently that of unity of place. The spectator's pleasure, he maintains, is increased by the observance of these two rules since 'sans aucune peine ou distraction il voit ici les choses comme si véritablement elles arrivaient devant lui', whereas if the action lasts for ten or twelve years,

il faut de nécessité que l'imagination soit divertie du plaisir de ce spectacle qu'elle considérait comme présent, et qu'elle travaille à comprendre comme quoi le même acteur qui naguère parlait à Rome à la dernière scène du premier acte, à la première du second se trouve dans la ville d'Athènes, ou dans le grand Caire si vous voulez; il est impossible que l'imagination ne se refroidisse, et qu'une si soudaine mutation de scène ne la surprenne et ne la dégoûte extrêmement, s'il faut qu'elle coure toujours après son objet de province en province et que presque en un moment elle passe les monts et traverse les mers avec lui.[2]

Throughout the 1630s playwrights gradually tended to observe the three unities, but there was a good deal of resistance and the change only came very slowly. In 1630, in the preface to his highly irregular tragicomedy, *La Généreuse Allemande*, André Mareschal declared that he had no intention of limiting himself ' à ces étroites bornes ni du lieu, ni du temps, ni de l'action'. The supporters of the rules he treats with contemptuous defiance when he writes:

Qu'ils me soutiennent que le sujet de théâtre doit être un en l'action, c'est-à-dire être simple en son événement et ne recevoir d'incidents qui ne tendent tous à un seul effet d'une personne seule, je leur déclarerai que le mien en a deux diverses. Qu'ils soutiennent encore que la scène ne connaît qu'un lieu et que pour faire quelque rapport du spectacle aux spectateurs qui ne remuent point, elle n'en peut sortir qu'en même temps elle ne sorte aussi de la raison, j'avouerai que la mienne, du commencement et pendant

---

[1] *Théâtre du XVIIe siècle*, ed. J. Scherer (Paris, 1975–), vol. i, p. 479.
[2] Ibid., p. 484.

les deux premiers actes, est en la ville de Prague, et presque tout le reste en celle d'Aule, en un mot qu'elle passe de Bohême en Silésie. De plus qu'ils jurent qu'un sujet, pour être juste, ne doit contenir d'actions qui s'étendent au delà d'un jour et qui ne puissent avoir été faites entre deux soleils, je ne suis pas pour cela prêt à croire que celles que j'ai décrites et qui sont véritables, pour avoir franchi ces limites aient plus mauvaise grâce.

Georges de Scudéry, who was later to attack *Le Cid* for its relatively minor violations of the rules, began his career as a playwright around 1630 with a series of highly irregular tragicomedies. In 1631 in the preface to the first of these, *Ligdamon et Lidias*, he emphatically rejects the three unities: 'J'ai voulu me dispenser de ces bornes trop étroites, faisant changer aussi souvent de face à mon théâtre que les acteurs y changent de lieu; chose qui, selon mon sentiment, a plus d'éclat que la vieille comédie.'[1]

However, the general trend towards the observance of the unities in the 1630s was unmistakable. Sometimes, it is true, they were only loosely observed. Unity of place, as in *Le Cid*, was taken to cover a number of places inside one town, while, again as in *Le Cid*, playwrights observing unity of time often tended to cram an improbable number of events into the space of twenty-four hours. In Mairet's tragicomedy, *Virginie*, performed in the theatrical year 1632/33, a naïve remark put into the mouth of one of the characters clumsily underlines the large number of incidents which the author had accumulated in this short space of time:

> Dieu! en ce peu de temps qu'enferment deux soleils
> Peut-il bien arriver des accidents[2] pareils?[3]

Looking back on his earlier career as a playwright, Corneille was to argue that, particularly when a fairly large number of events were crowded into a play like *Le Cid*, it would be better if the period of time were simply left to the spectator's imagination instead of being repeatedly indicated in the course of the play. 'Qu'est-il besoin', he asks, 'de remarquer à l'ouverture du théâtre que le soleil se lève, qu'il est midi au troisième acte, et qu'il se couche à la fin du dernier? C'est une affectation qui ne fait qu'importuner.'[4]

---

[1] The drama of the Ancients.
[2] Striking events.　　　　　[3] Act V, sc. 2.
[4] *Writings on the Theatre*, ed. H. T. Barnwell (Oxford, 1965), p. 73.

Important as the rule of the three unities was, excessive stress on it leads one to look merely at the mechanics of Classical drama, particularly tragedy, and to ignore the result achieved by its observance. The adoption of the unities of time and place brought about the creation of a particular type of tragedy, one in which physical action is subordinated to psychological conflict portrayed at a moment of crisis. It is the content of Classical tragedy—the psychological conflict, the concentration on a crisis—which is more important than the formal details of the rule of the three unities.

Moreover, the unities were far from being the only rules governing French Classical tragedy. Two other principles to which the theorists of the time attached great importance were those of *vraisemblance* ('verisimilitude') and *les bienséances* ('the proprieties'). Neither of these terms is as easily defined as a clear-cut rule like that of the three unities; though the seventeenth-century theorists and playwrights continually used these two terms, unfortunately they did not define them with any great precision for the benefit of posterity. Yet in view of their importance the student of the drama of the age has to make an effort to grasp what they understood by them.

Both theorists and playwrights constantly stress the necessity for *vraisemblance*. When in the preface to *Bérénice* Racine wrote: 'Il n'y a que le vraisemblable qui touche dans la tragédie', he was merely stating one of the great commonplaces of the age. Abbé d'Aubignac's *Pratique du théâtre* is crammed full of allusions to the importance of the principle, and the chapter headed 'De la Vraisemblance' opens with the sweeping statement: 'Voici le fondement de toutes les pièces de théâtre; chacun en parle et peu de gens l'entendent. Voici le caractère général auquel il faut reconnaître tout ce qui s'y passe. En un mot, la vraisemblance est, s'il le faut ainsi dire, l'essence du poème dramatique et sans laquelle il ne se peut rien faire ni rien dire de raisonnable sur la scène.' [1] It is true that at first sight Corneille appears to be somewhat of a heretic in the midst of this chorus of voices in favour of *vraisemblance*. In 1647 in the preface to his tragedy, *Héraclius*, he declares: 'Je ne craindrai point d'avancer que le sujet d'une belle tragédie doit n'être pas vraisemblable.' Critics

[1] *La Pratique de théâtre*, p. 76.

have sometimes seized on this statement and made out of it the very essence of Corneille's conception of tragedy, contrasting it with that of other playwrights of the age and particularly Racine, but this 'paradoxe' as he himself calls it is not an exact expression of his ideas. In his *Discours sur le poème dramatique* he puts the point more soberly when he writes: '. . . On en est venu jusqu'à établir une maxime très fausse, qu'*il faut que le sujet d'une tragédie soit vraisemblable*; . . . les grands sujets qui remuent les passions et en opposent l'impétuosité aux lois du devoir ou aux tendresses du sang, doivent toujours aller au-delà du vraisemblable.' [1] In other words he tones down somewhat his earlier statement and no longer maintains that the subject of a tragedy *must* be *invraisemblable*, but merely that this is the kind which he prefers.

If this view inevitably diminishes the amount of *vraisemblance* in Corneille's plays, it has to be borne in mind that in any tragedies of the period, including those of Racine, with whom Corneille is so often contrasted, the amount of *vraisemblance* is necessarily relative. In fact this tremendous stress on the necessity for *vraisemblance* in the writings of the theorists and playwrights of seventeenth-century France involves them in all sorts of contradictions.

In the controversy about the three unities which took place around 1630 both sides made use of the principle, some to demand observance of the unities, others to reject them. Indeed strict observance of the unities of time and place was bound to lead to a clash with *vraisemblance*. In early Classical tragedies such as Mairet's *Sophonisbe* and Corneille's *Le Cid* an extraordinary number of events are crammed into the space of a mere twenty-four hours. If it is true that from the 1640s onwards most authors of tragedies reduced substantially the number of events forced into the space of one day, observance of unity of place continued to lead to an obvious clash with *vraisemblance,* in the plays of Racine as much as in any others. There is clearly considerable improbability that all the scenes of a play should take place in one room in a palace. Although the strict observance of these two unities inevitably led to *invraisemblance*, they were accepted in the seventeenth century as dramatic conventions.

[1] *Writings on the Theatre*, pp. 1-2.

A clash was also inevitable between *vraisemblance* and historical truth. In his *Art poétique* Boileau penned the famous couplet:

> Jamais au spectateur n'offrez rien d'incroyable.
> Le vrai peut quelquefois n'être pas vraisemblable.[1]

Then which principle was one to follow? It was natural that Corneille, given his somewhat independent views on the subject of *vraisemblance*, should answer critics of his plays by retorting that what they found *invraisemblable* was historically true. Like his contemporaries, however, he also held that the playwright was justified in altering or adding to the historical or legendary data on which his tragedy was based in order to conform to the principle of *vraisemblance*.

Racine for his part, despite his allegiance to this principle, devotes a great deal of space in his prefaces to arguing that this or that detail in his tragedies which had been attacked by the critics has a definite source in history or legend. In the second preface to his early tragedy, *Alexandre*, he declares: 'Il n'y a guère de tragédie où l'histoire soit plus fidèlement suivie que dans celle-ci', this despite the fact that he had entirely invented not only his central character, Axiane, but also a brother-and-sister relationship for two others. In the second preface to *Andromaque* he justifies the way he has prolonged the life of Astyanax, the son of Hector and Andromache, on the grounds that 'nos vieilles chroniques sauvent la vie à ce jeune prince,après la désolation de son pays, pour en faire le fondateur de notre monarchie'. Often he goes to the most obscure sources to justify some feature in his tragedies. Thus in the preface to *Britannicus* he answers the critics who claimed that 'd'une vieille coquette, nommée Junia Silana, j'en ai fait une jeune fille très sage' by the retort: 'S'ils avaient bien lu l'histoire, ils auraient trouvé une Junia Calvina, de la famille d'Auguste.' When he invented characters, as here or in the case of Aricie in *Phèdre*, he always seeks out some authority who at least mentions such a name. In the preface to *Phèdre* he writes: 'Cette Aricie n'est point un personage de mon invention. Virgile dit qu'Hippolyte l'épousa, et en eut un fils, après qu'Esculape l'eut ressuscité.' This constant

---

[1] *Œuvres complètes*, p.170.

recourse to the principle of historical or legendary truth is not easily reconciled with the importance which Racine along with other writers of the time attached to *vraisemblance*.

In practice despite the stress which was laid on the concept of *vraisemblance* by the theorists, despite the lip-service paid to it by the playwrights of the age, this rule was almost more honoured in the breach than in the observance. Classical tragedies are full of *invraisemblances*, conscious or unconscious. After all the principle is an extemely vague one; the very expression 'what seems to be true' is ambiguous. Who is to judge 'what seems to be true'? 'Le vraisemblable', declared Father Rapin in his *Réflexions sur la poétique* which appeared in 1674, in the same year as Boileau's *Art poétique*, 'est tout ce qui est conforme à l'opinion du public.'[1] But what is the audience but a mass of individuals with very different ideas of 'what seems to be true'?

Observance of the *bienséances* is another extremely important principle in the dramatic theory of the age, but it must be said that, although the expression is constantly used by both critics and playwrights, not only do they nowhere define it with any sort of precision, but they also tend to confuse it to some extent with the principle of *vraisemblance*.

Broadly speaking, the observance of the *bienséances* required that a play should not conflict with the tastes and moral outlook or prejudices of the audience.

It is clear that this principle must to some extent clash with that of preserving historical or legendary truth, and in practice playwrights were often compelled to alter the historical or legendary data on which their tragedies were based so as not to come into conflict with the taste and moral outlook of their age.

From the 1630s onwards plays, even comedies, began gradually to become much more chaste than they had earlier been. The change was naturally quite slow. Plays written in that decade often contained situations and used language which would have shocked later in the century. In this connection it is interesting that in later versions of his early comedies Corneille toned down certain situations and expressions in order to conform with the *bienséances*. The new importance which was being increasingly

[1] *Réflexions sur la poétique,* ed. E. T. Dubois (Paris and Geneva, 1970), p. 39.

attached to the principle is well brought out by the controversy over the behaviour of Chimène in *Le Cid*. This was denounced by Georges de Scudéry as 'impudique' and he declared that the play was 'de très mauvais exemple': 'L'on y voit une fille dénaturée ne parler que de ses folies, lorsqu'elle ne doit parler que de son malheur; plaindre la perte de son amant, lorsqu'elle ne doit songer qu'à celle de son père; aimer encore ce qu'elle doit abhorrer; souffrir en même temps, et en même maison, ce meurtrier et ce pauvre corps; et, pour achever son impiété, joindre sa main à celle qui dégoutte encore du sang de son père.'[1] This view was solemnly echoed in the verdict on poor Chimène given in the *Sentiments de l'Académie française sur le 'Cid'*: 'Ses mœurs sont du moins scandaleuses si en effet elles ne sont dépravées.'[2]

One could quote innumerable examples of the way in which authors of Classical tragedies altered the facts of history or legend in order not to shock the taste of their contemporaries. The historical relationship between the two main characters of Corneille's *Nicomède*—the hero and his father, Prusias—was that Prusias intended to kill his son, but was in the end killed by him. This was obviously too shocking. Corneille, as he tells us in his *Avis au lecteur*, entirely changed the ending of his play. 'J'ai ôté de ma scène l'horreur d'une catastrophe si barbare, et n'ai donné ni au père ni au fils aucun dessein de parricide.'[3] Another well-known example is furnished by the *Examen* of his *Œdipe* where he declares that to depict on the stage certain episodes in the Oedipus legend as portrayed by Sophocles and Seneca would have been too strong meat for theatre-goers of his day, particularly the ladies: '. . . Cette éloquente et sérieuse description de la manière dont ce malheureux prince se crève les yeux, qui occupe tout leur cinquième acte, ferait soulever la délicatesse de nos dames, dont le dégoût attire aisément celui du reste de l'auditoire.' Corneille had had his difficulties with the *bienséances*, not only over Chimène in *Le Cid*, but also over his religious tragedy, *Théodore vierge et martyre*, the failure of which was due, he was assured by contemporary critics, 'à l'idée

---

[1] *La Querelle du 'Cid'*, p. 80.   [2] Ibid., p. 372.
[3] The word had a very wide sense, covering the murder of any near relative or even of a king.

de la prostitution, qu'on n'a pu souffrir, bien qu'on sût assez qu'elle n'avait point d'effet, et que, pour en exténuer l'horreur, j'ai employé tout ce que l'art et l'expérience m'ont pu fournir de lumières.' The *Examen* of the play continues with the ironical sentence: 'Dans cette disgrâce,[1] j'ai de quoi congratuler à la pureté de notre scène, de voir qu'une histoire qui fait le plus bel ornement du second livre des *Vierges* de saint Ambroise, se trouve trop licencieuse pour y être supportée.' In other words, in neither case was the plea that he was merely following his sources regarded as acceptable.

Equally striking examples of changes made in order to observe the *bienséances* are to be found in the tragedies of Racine. In *Mithridate*, for instance, he makes the Greek princess, Monime, the king's fiancée whereas, historically speaking, she was one of the numerous wives in his harem. In *Phèdre* he does not follow the Ancients in making the heroine accuse Hippolytus herself; he explains in the preface that he has transferred the blame for his action to her *nourrice*, Œnone: 'J'ai cru que la calomnie avait quelque chose de trop bas et de trop noir pour la mettre dans la bouche d'une princesse qui a d'ailleurs des sentiments si nobles et si vertueux. Cette bassesse m'a semblé plus convenable à une nourrice . . .' He goes on to mention another significant change which he had made in the legendary data on which his play was based: 'Hippolyte est accusé, dans Euripide et dans Sénèque, d'avoir en effet violé sa belle-mère: *Vim corpus tulit.* Mais il n'est ici accusé que d'en avoir eu le dessein.'

A study of seventeenth-century plays show a gradual trend towards ever-increasing refinement. Words, expressions, situations tolerated on the stage in the opening decades of the period were gradually proscribed as contrary to the *bienséances*. Indecent words, expressions, and situations were not the only victims of the *bienséances*. While details of ordinary, everyday things continued to abound in comedy as it dealt with contemporary life, they were banished from tragedy. Such matters as eating, drinking, sleeping, or being ill were considered to be beneath the dignity of this type of drama. In a Racine tragedy the mention that a female character has been dressed, has had her hair done, and has neither slept nor eaten for three days is

[1] 'Misfortune'.

most carefully wrapped up in elegant periphrases. On her first appearance Phèdre is made to exclaim:

> Que ces vains ornements, que ces voiles me pèsent!
> Quelle importune main, en formant tous ces nœuds,
> A pris soin sur mon front d'assembler mes cheveux?

To which her *nourrice* adds further details on her mistress's distraught state:

> Les ombres par trois fois ont obscurci les cieux
> Depuis que le sommeil n'est entré dans vos yeux;
> Et le jour a trois fois chassé la nuit obscure
> Depuis que votre corps languit sans nourriture.

And these precautions, it will be noted, have been taken to state the fact that Phèdre has *not* slept and *not* eaten.

The *bienséances* also ruled out the depiction on the stage of all forms of violent action such as duels, battles, and murders. Battles faded out early in the century. Duels took rather longer; though in *Le Cid* the duel between Rodrigue and the count is kept off the stage, the spectator is allowed to see the short one in which the father is disarmed. Until about 1640 murders were quite common on the stage, and the most grisly tortures and deaths continued to be described in *récits* until even later. However, by about the middle of the century such horrible details had been banished from *récits* as well as from the stage. Any murder was carefully removed out of the spectator's sight, as in Corneille's *Horace* where it is made clear that the hero pursues his sister, Camille, off the stage and that she is 'blessée derrière le théâtre'. In his *Examen* of the play Corneille makes this quite explicit when, after frankly admitting that the killing of Camille is a weakness of the play, he goes on to say: 'On l'attribue communément à ce qu'on voit cette mort sur la scène; ce qui serait plutôt la faute de l'actrice que la mienne, parce que, quand elle voit son frère mettre l'épée à la main, la frayeur, si naturelle au sexe, lui doit faire prendre la fuite, et recevoir le coup derrière le théâtre, comme je le marque dans cette impression.'

On the other hand suicide continued to be tolerated on the stage, as the example of the ending of *Phèdre* shows. It will be noticed, however, that Racine conforms to the usual practice of the time by placing Phèdre's death from poison in the very last scene of his tragedy; this avoids cluttering up the stage with a corpse or corpses.

The rules of the unities, *vraisemblance*, and *bienséances* do not by any means exhaust the list of those laid down for drama in the 1630s and 1640s. All sorts of technical details, major and minor, were regulated in great detail. For instance, tragedies had to be in five acts, though there was always a much greater variety of length in comedy where plays in three acts and especially in one act were common. Inside each of the acts the scenes had to be linked; this rule of the *liaison des scènes* required that the stage must never be left empty in the course of an act. In other words, at least one character had to remain on the stage at the end of a scene and take part in the one which followed. An exception was allowed for what was known as *liaison de fuite*. A good example of this is provided by Act IV of *Andromaque* (sc.s 1-2) where, with the words 'C'est Hermione. Allons, fuyons sa violence', Andromaque, followed by her *confidente*, leaves the stage to be occupied by Hermione and Cléone. *Liaison des scènes* obviously implied the observance of unity of place. It is breached, as Corneille has to admit in his *Examen* of the play, in the fourth act of *Cinna* when we are shown in succession the Emperor and Empress in their apartment in the palace, followed by Émilie with her *confidente* in hers. The difficulty in which Corneille found himself over observing the rule in this play arose out of his failure to observe strict unity of place as he requires two apartments in the palace instead of one for all the scenes in his tragedy.

According to the rules the dénouement of a play must arise out of the data supplied to the audience in the exposition; it must dispose of all the main characters and yet at the same time be as rapid as possible. The ending of a Classical tragedy was generally unhappy. That is, on paper at least, what distinguished it from a tragicomedy according to the definitions of the two genres provided by Chappuzeau: 'La tragédie est une représentation grave et sérieuse d'une action funeste, qui s'est passée entre des personnes que leur grande qualité ou leur grand mérite relèvent au-dessus des personnes communes, et le plus souvent c'est entre des princes et des rois.[1] La tragi-comédie nous met

[1] Comedy in the view of the theorists dealt with lesser mortals. Chappuzeau defines it thus: 'La comédie est une représentation naïve et enjouée d'une aventure agréable entre des personnes communes, à quoi l'on ajoute souvent la douce satire pour la correction des mœurs.'

devant les yeux de nobles aventures entre d'illustres personnes menacées de quelque grande infortune, qui se trouve suivie d'un heureux événement.'[1] A tragedy need not necessarily end bloodily as Racine made clear in the preface to *Bérénice*: 'Ce n'est point une nécessité qu'il y ait du sang et des morts dans une tragédie; il suffit que l'action en soit grande, que les acteurs en soient héroïques,[2] que les passions y soient excitées, et que tout s'y ressente de cette tristesse majestueuse qui fait tout le plaisir de la tragédie.'

It is, however, somewhat disconcerting to find that certain well-known tragedies of the period have a happy ending. In the final scene of Corneille's *Cinna* the emperor Augustus not only pardons the conspirators who had planned to assassinate him, but also heaps favours upon them, while in Racine's *Iphigénie* the main character is saved at the very last moment from becoming a sacrifical victim because, as Racine puts it in the preface, 'quelle apparence que j'eusse souillé la scène par le meurtre horrible d'une personne aussi vertueuse et aussi aimable qu'il fallait représenter Iphigénie?'

One has to bear in mind that the theorists of the time did recognize a second type of tragedy, one with a happy ending. In an age when the principle of the imitation of the Ancients was widely accepted, they invoke, as might be expected, their authority for this kind of ending. Writing in 1639 (before Corneille produced his *Cinna*) in his *Discours sur la tragédie* Sarasin boldly declares: 'Aristote . . . met l'issue heureuse parmi le dénombrement des fins de la tragédie', and he continues: 'Et quoique la plupart des tragédies versent du sang sur la scène et s'achèvent par quelque mort, il ne faut pas pour cela conclure que la fin de tous ces poèmes doive être funeste.'[3] Basing himself, he alleges, on the example furnished by certain plays of the Ancients, d'Aubignac likewise maintains that modern tragedies may have two very different types of ending, since they 'finissent toujours, ou par l'infortune des principaux personnages ou par une prospérité telle qu'ils l'avaient pu souhaiter'. He goes on to develop the point further: '. . . Plusieurs se sont imaginé que le mot

---

[1] *Le Théâtre français*, p. 25 (*événement* = 'issue, outcome').
[2] 'Illustrious'.
[3] *Œuvres*, ed. P. Festugière (Paris, 1926, 2 vols.), vol. ii, p. 33.

tragique ne signifiait jamais qu'une aventure funeste et sanglante, et qu'un poème dramatique ne pouvait être nommé *tragédie* si la catastrophe ne contenait la mort ou l'infortune des principaux personnages; mais c'est à tort . . . Aussi voyons-nous que des dix-neuf tragédies d'Euripide, il y en a un grand nombre dont l'issue est heureuse . . .'[1] For the *Concise Oxford Dictionary* a tragedy is a 'drama . . . with unhappy events or ending', but this is certainly not necessarily true of a seventeenth-century *tragédie*.

On paper the theorists of the period agreed that it was desirable to bring as much as possible of the action on to the stage. In the very pugnacious first preface to *Britannicus*, replying to critics who had objected to the final appearance of Junie at the end of the play (a scene he subsequently suppressed), Racine makes the retort: 'Ils ne savent pas qu'une des règles du théâtre est de ne mettre en récit que les choses qui ne se peuvent passer en action.' In practice the rules of the three unities, *vraisemblance*, and the *bienséances* often made it impossible to do so. Hence the frequency in Classical tragedy of *récits* in which events that take place off stage are related to the audience by one of the characters—much to the disgust of Victor Hugo who argued that, if Racine had not been hamstrung by the rules, 'il n'eût pas . . . relégué dans la coulisse cette admirable scène du banquet où l'élève de Sénèque empoisonne Britannicus dans la coupe de la réconciliation'.[2] Classical practice is well summed up in Boileau's lines:

> Ce qu'on ne doit point voir, qu'un récit nous l'expose:
> Les yeux en le voyant saisiraient mieux la chose,
> Mais il est des objets que l'art judicieux
> Doit offrir à l'oreille et reculer des yeux.[3]

Elaborate rules were laid down by the theorists for the *récit*: rather obviously, a character must not relate to the spectator things he already knows; the person who relates the events must have a strong reason for doing so, and the person to whom he relates them must have good reason to listen. It was generally held that such *récits* were best placed at either the beginning or end of a play.

There were also strict rules concerning the language to be used

---

[1] *La Pratique du théâtre*, pp. 136, 143.
[2] *Théâtre complet*, vol. i, p. 432.   [3] *Œuvres complètes*, p. 170.

in drama, particularly in tragedy. This required a language stripped of all ordinary, realistic terms drawn from everyday life. 'Nous voulons', wrote La Mesnardière in *La Poétique*,[1] 'que la tragédie parle majestueusement, qu'elle emploie les belles paroles, les locutions magnifiques, et qu'elle chasse loin de soi tout ce qui ressent la bassesse et les façons populaires.' 'La diction', declared Father Rapin, 'doit être noble et relevée . . . car tout ce qui est commun et ordinaire dans les termes ne lui est pas propre. Il faut des paroles qui n'aient rien de bas et de vulgaire, une diction noble et magnifique.'[2] There was naturally a wide gap between the 'style noble' of tragedy and the more everyday language to be found in the comedies of the period, since the latter genre was generally regarded as an inferior one by the theorists, and it was allowed a great deal of freedom, indeed licence, to enable it to portray contemporary life. 'Néanmoins', Father Rapin declares, 'les termes bas et vulgaires ne doivent pas être permis sur le théâtre s'ils ne sont soutenus de quelque sorte d'esprit. Les proverbes et les bons mots du peuple n'y doivent pas aussi être soufferts s'ils n'ont quelque sens plaisant et s'ils ne sont naturels.'[3]

Such, in broad outline, were the famous rules as they related to drama. Worked out by the theorists and gradually adopted by the playwrights in the 1630s and 1640s, they slowly transformed French drama, particularly tragedy; there is an extraordinary gulf between the tragedies written before 1630, those of Alexandre Hardy for instance, and those written after that date. Naturally this evolution took place over a period of time, slowly working itself out by about the middle of the century. The 1630s and 1640s were a period of transition. Corneille and the other playwrights of his generation were feeling their way with the new dramatic technique which the rules imposed.

The once accepted contrast between Racine who, beginning his career a whole generation later, observed the rules naturally and effortlessly, and Corneille who was hampered by them, is misleading. Like his contemporaries Corneille gradually came to adopt the rules—with many hesitations and subtle reservations, it is true—but he did finally accept them because he felt that this

---

[1] Paris, 1640, p. 390.
[2] *Les Réflexions sur la poétique*, pp. 47–8.   [3] Ibid., p. 116.

was what the theatre-going public wanted. It is true that he always insisted that a writer must enjoy a certain freedom which might on occasion take him beyond the rules since the main object of any practising playwright must be to produce works which would give pleasure to the public and attract crowds of spectators to the theatre. The point is put very bluntly in the dedication to his comedy, *La Suivante*, published in 1637:

Puisque nous faisons des poèmes pour être représentés, notre premier but doit être de plaire à la cour et au peuple, et d'attirer un grand monde à leurs représentations. Il faut, s'il se peut, y ajouter les règles, afin de ne déplaire pas aux savants, et recevoir un applaudissement universel; mais surtout gagnons la voix publique; autrement, notre pièce aura beau être régulière, si elle est sifflée au théâtre, les savants n'oseront se déclarer en notre faveur, et aimeront mieux dire que nous aurons mal entendu les règles, que de nous donner des louanges quand nous serons décriés par le consentement général de ceux qui ne voient la comédie que pour se divertir.

This was a fairly early and somewhat brash statement of his attitude to the rules, but it is interesting to see that in the *Examen* of *Le Cid*, published over twenty years later, while he feels bound to admit that the two visits which Rodrigue makes to Chimène's house after killing her father are clean contrary to the *bienséances*, he none the less defends these scenes because of the effect they had on the audience: 'J'ai remarqué aux premières représentations qu'alors que ce malheureux amant se présentait devant elle, il s'élevait un certain frémissement dans l'assemblée, qui marquait une curiosité merveilleuse et un redoublement d'attention pour ce qu'ils avaient à se dire dans un état si pitoyable.' In other words, however contrary to the rules such scenes might be, they were highly effective on the stage, and that for Corneille was the really important thing.

Nor would the actor-playwright Molière or even Racine have disagreed with him. In *La Critique de l'École des femmes*, while declaring that his comedy does observe the rules laid down by the *savants*, Molière appeals over their heads to the ordinary theatre-goer when he plays down the importance of these prescriptions in the well-known passage put into the mouth of his spokesman, Dorante:

Vous êtes de plaisantes gens avec vos règles, dont vous embarrassez les ignorants et nous étourdissez tous les jours. Il semble, à vous ouïr parler, que ces règles de l'art soient les plus grands mystères du monde; et cependant ce ne sont que quelques observations aisées, que le bon sens a faites sur ce qui peut ôter le plaisir que l'on prend à ces sortes de poèmes; et le même bon sens qui a fait autrefois ces observations les fait aisément tous les jours sans le secours d'Horace et d'Aristote.

Though the rules have their place, they are none the less subordinated to a higher rule—to give pleasure to the spectator, or, to quote the words which Molière puts into the mouth of Dorante, 'Je voudrais bien savoir si la grande règle de toutes les règles n'est pas de plaire, et si une pièce de théâtre qui a attrapé son but n'a pas suivi un bon chemin.'

The same attitude to the rules is shown even by Racine. In the preface to *Bérénice* he replies to the objection of some theatre-goers who, while admitting that his tragedy had given them pleasure, expressed doubts as to whether the extreme simplicity of action in his play was in accordance with the rules:

On me dit qu'ils avouaient tous qu'elle n'ennuyait point, qu'elle les touchait même en plusieurs endroits et qu'ils la verraient encore avec plaisir. Que veulent-ils davantage? Je les conjure d'avoir assez bonne opinion d'eux-mêmes pour ne pas croire qu'une pièce qui les touche et qui leur donne du plaisir puisse être absolument contre les règles. La principale règle est de plaire et de toucher. Toutes les autres ne sont faites que pour parvenir à cette première. Mais toutes ces règles sont d'un long détail dont je ne leur conseille pas de s'embarrasser. Ils ont des occupations plus importantes. Qu'ils se reposent sur nous de la fatigue d'éclaircir les difficultés de la *Poétique* d'Aristote; qu'ils se réservent le plaisir de pleurer et d'être attendris . . .

Racine in tragedy with 'La principale règle est de plaire et de toucher' echoes Molière in comedy and his 'La grande règle de toutes les règles est de plaire'.

Thus although such theorists as Chapelain and Sarasin, La Mesnardière and d'Aubignac did exercise a very considerable influence on the development of French drama from the 1630s onwards, that influence came up against decided limits. The playwrights of the time, including the very greatest of them, had to bear in mind that the spectators for whom they were writing—the men and women of the court, of Paris high society, and of the middle classes—came to the theatre, not to see whether their plays observed the rules laid down by the *savants*, but to be entertained. Corneille, Molière, and Racine all agree that above all the detailed rules prescribed by the theorists there is the higher rule of giving pleasure to the spectator.

Conclusion

In some quarters today it is fashionable to study works of literature in complete isolation from the age and the society in which they were written. This method is peculiarly inappropriate when applied to the drama of any period since it has always been so eminently a social art, relying on the collaboration of playwright, actor, and audience. The plays of any seventeenth-century French writer, whether they be those of an actor-playwright like Molière or of authors like Corneille and Racine who had made writing their profession, can only be understood if one has some knowledge of the conditions (and the constraints) under which they produced their works. Certain characteristics of the drama of their age derive from moral, social, and material conditions peculiar to seventeenth-century France and different in many respects from those of today. To know in a certain amount of detail what those conditions were is a decided help towards appreciating the greatness of men like Corneille, Molière and Racine.

Two other aids to such an appreciation are also important. In reading the plays of the period and their prefaces one has constantly to be alert to the pitfalls produced by linguistic change. A large number of French words in use in both the seventeenth and the twentieth centuries have undergone considerable changes of meaning in the course of some three hundred years; the word *comédie* is only one example out of many. Again, as virtually all tragedies and many comedies were written in verse, it is essential to acquire a grasp of the basic principles of French versification, particularly of the alexandrine, in order to appreciate the mastery of it shown by the great playwrights of the age. However, these are topics too large to be more than touched on in a conclusion which, like the rest of the book, has deliberately been kept short.

Bibliography

Adam. A. *Théophile de Viau et la libre pensée française en 1620.* Paris 1935.

Argenson, M.R. de V. d'. *Notes*, ed. L.Larchey and E. Mabille. Paris, 1866.

Aubignac, abbé d'. *La Pratique du théâtre*, ed. P. Martino. Algiers–Paris, 1927.

    Dissertation sur la condamnation des théâtres. Paris, 1666.

Baillet, A. *Jugements des savants.* 8 vols. Amsterdam, 1725.

Benserade, I. de. *Œuvres.* 2 vols. Paris, 1697.

Bentley, G. E. *The Jacobean and Caroline Stage. Dramatic Companies and Players.* 2 vols. Oxford, 1941.

Boileau, N. *Œuvres complètes*, ed. A. Adam. Paris, 1966.

Bourdel, N. 'L'Établissement et la construction de l'Hôtel des Comédiens Français rue des Fossés-Saint-Germain-des-Prés (Ancienne Comédie) 1687–1690', *Revue d'histoire du théâtre*, 1955.

Boursault, E. *Artémise et Poliante.* Paris, 1670.

    Lettres nouvelles. 3 vols. Paris, 1722.

Browne, E. *A Journal of a Visit to Paris in the year 1664*, ed. G. Keynes. London, 1923.

Campardon, E. *Documents inédits sur J.B. Poquelin Molière.* Paris, 1871.

    Les Comédiens du Roi de la Troupe française pendant les deux derniers siècles. Paris, 1879.

Chapelain, J. *Lettres*, ed. P. Tamizey de Larroque. 2 vols. Paris, 1880.

    Opuscules critiques, ed. A.C. Hunter. Paris, 1936.

Chappuzeau, S. *Le Théâtre français*, ed. G. Monval. Paris, 1876.

Chevalley, S. *Album Théâtre classique. La Vie théâtrale sous Louis XIII et Louis XIV.* Paris, 1970.

Corneille, P. *Œuvres complètes*, ed. C. Marty-Laveaux. 12 vols. Paris, 1868.

    Writings on the Theatre, ed. H. T. Barnwell, Oxford, 1965.

Dangeau, P. de. *Journal*, ed. E. Soulié *et al.* 19 vols. Paris, 1854–60.

Deierkauf-Holsboer, S.W. *Vie d'Alexandre Hardy, poète du roi, 1572–1632.* New edition, Paris, 1972.

    Le Théâtre du Marais. 2 vols. Paris, 1954–8.

    Le Théâtre de l'Hôtel de Bourgogne. 2 vols. Paris, 1968–70.

Dubu, J. 'De quelques rituels des diocèses de France au XVIIe siècle et du théâtre,' *L'Année canonique*, 1957.

François de Sales. *Introduction à la vie dévote.* 3rd edition, Lyons, 1610.

G. Guéret. *La Promenade de Saint-Cloud* in F. Bruys, *Mémoires historiques, critiques et littéraires.* 2 vols. Paris, 1751.

Hubert, A. *Registre 1672-1673*, ed. S. Chevalley, *Revue d'histoire du théâtre*, 1973.

Heuzey, J. 'Du costume et de la décoration tragique au XVIIe siècle', *Revue d'histoire du théâtre*, 1960.

Hugo, V. *Théâtre complet*, ed. R. Purnal *et al.* 2 vols. Paris, 1967–9.

Jal, A. *Dictionnaire critique de biographie et d'histoire*. 2nd edition, Paris, 1872.

Jurgens, M. and Maxfield-Miller, M. *Cent ans de recherches sur Molière*. Paris, 1963.

La Grange, C. V. de. *Registre (1659-1685)*, ed. B. E. and G. P. Young. 2 vols. Paris, 1947.

Lamare, N. de. *Traité de la police*. 4 vols. Paris, 1705–38.

La Mesnardière, H.J.P. de. *La Poétique*. Paris, 1640.

Lancaster, H. C. *The Comédie Française, 1680-1701: Plays, Actors, Spectators, Finances*. Baltimore, 1941.

L'Estoile, P. de. *Mémoires-journaux*, ed. G. Brunet *et al.* 12 vols. Paris, 1875–96.

Loret, J. *La Muse historique*, ed. C. Livet. 4 vols. Paris, 1857–78.

Martin, H.J. *Livre, pouvoirs et société à Paris au XVIIe siècle*. Paris, 1969.

Le Mémoire de Mahelot, Laurent et d'autres décorateurs de l'Hôtel de Bourgogne et de la Comédie Française au XVIIe siècle, ed. H. C. Lancaster. Paris, 1920.

Mercier, L. S. *Tableau de Paris*. 12 vols. Amsterdam, 1783–9.

Mongrédien, G. *Recueil des textes et des documents du XVIIe siècle relatifs à Molière*. 2 vols. Paris, 1965.

    La Vie quotidienne des comédiens au temps de Molière. Paris, 1966.

    Dictionnaire biographique des comédiens français du XVIIe siècle. Paris, 1961,

    and Robert, J. *Supplément au Dictionnaire biographique des comédiens français du XVIIe siècle*. Paris, 1971.

Monval, G. 'André Mareschal', *Le Moliériste*, vol. ix.

Parfaict, C. and F. *Histoire du théâtre français depuis son origine jusqu'à présent*. 15 vols. Amsterdam and Paris, 1735–49.

La Querelle du 'Cid', ed. A. Gasté. Paris, 1898.

Quinault, P. *Théâtre*. 5 vols. Paris, 1715.

Racine, J. *Œuvres complètes*, ed. R. Picard. 2 vols. Paris 1950–2.

Racine, L. *Œuvres*. 4 vols. Paris, 1743–7.

Rapin, R. *Réflexions sur la poétique*, ed. E. T. Dubois, Geneva–Paris, 1970.

Saint-Simon, duc de. *Mémoires*, ed. A. de Boislisle. 43 vols. Paris, 1879–1930.

Sarasin, J. P. *Œuvres*, ed. P. Festugière. 2 vols. Paris, 1926.

Scarron, P. *Poésies diverses*, ed. M. Cauchie. 2 vols. Paris, 1947–61.

Schelandre, J. de. *Tyr et Sidon, tragédie, et Tyr et Sidon, tragi-comédie*, ed. J. W. Barker. Paris, 1975.

Scherer, J. *La Dramaturgie classique en France*. Paris, 1950.

Scudéry, G. de. *Apologie du théâtre*. Paris, 1639.

Segrais, J. R. de. *Œuvres*. 2 vols. Paris, 1755.

Skippon, P. *An Account of a Journey through Part of the Low Countries, Germany, Italy and France* in *A Collection of Voyages and Travels*. Vol. vi. London, 1732.

Sorel, C. *La Maison des jeux*. 2 vols. Paris, 1642.

    Bibliothèque française. Paris, 1667.

    De la connaissance des bons livres. Amsterdam, 1672.

Tallemant des Réaux, G. *Historiettes*, ed. G. Mongrédien. 8 vols. Paris, 1932–4.

Théâtre du XVIIe siècle, ed. J. Scherer. Paris, 1975–.

Tralage, J. N. de. Recueil. Bibliothèque de l'Arsenal, MS.6544.

Urbain, C. and Levesque, E. *L'Église et le théâtre*. Paris, 1930.

Vaunois, L. *L'Enfance et la jeunesse de Racine*. Paris, 1964.

Voltaire, F. A. de. *Complete works*, ed. T. Besterman. Geneva, Banbury, and Oxford, 1968–.

Index